Book Cover by SW Global Publishing (Pty) Ltd
Editing by SW Global Publishing (Pty) Ltd

Photographs by Joe Brooks Photography

First edition 2023

ISBN: 978-0-6452371-8-4

Memories Made with Every Cup

A JOURNEY OF A MOTHER AND HER DAUGHTER

LEILA & ERIKA SHANOFF

Charlotte, our family matriarch...
Leila follows in her auspicious footprints!

Dedication

We dedicate our book to our beloved mother and grandmother, Charlotte. As we grew up, she was always there for us, always devoted to our family. Charlotte's passion for cooking was evident in all her homecooked meals and continues to inspire every plate of food we make. But mostly, her sense of humor and laughter echo in our hearts and are truly missed!

Erika dreams of one day owning her own Tea Room!

Memories Made with Every Cup – A Journey of a Mother and her Daughter

INTRODUCTION

Life is made up of special moments. If enough moments are strung together, they make a memory, and many great memories, like love, is what life is all about. Our tea room has so many memories; in fact, "Memories are Made with Every Cup!"

At the heart of all good stories is a strong foundation. Our foundation begins and ends with the bond between mother and daughter. A bond that cannot be compared with any other relationship in your life and can take on many forms. Not only are we mother and daughter, we are best friends, partners in our life's work, and often one mind working as two parts of a whole. Scary, right? We know...but sometimes that's just how it goes!

Erika says, "When I was just a little girl, I asked my mother what would I be when I got older. She had hoped that someday I would become a doctor or a lawyer, but never did she think that as we sat together enjoying a cup of Créme Brûlèe tea, that someday we would own our own tea room."

Life has a way of playing tricks on you. Leila says that Erika promised her an easy retirement after working in the financial arena for over thirty-five years. Leila's typical twelve-hour day running a small business credit area and in the trenches soliciting small business loans used brain power. Now, the twelve-hour days baking and cooking in Erika's Tea Room kitchen uses physical power. Leila has the Popeye muscles as evidence of this transition! Leila also loves the idea of being her own boss, not having to check in with a zillion bosses (slight exaggeration) she had to answer to. But not to worry, not much has changed. Erika loves to be Leila's boss when she can get away with it!

Erika loved teaching in the New Jersey school system, but after moving to Florida, learned that their schools were very different. She was asked to dumb down her lessons for teaching the teachers. *There are only a few words that rhyme with cat and hat*, she would say. So she jumped at the chance to retire from teaching. Again, the mother-daughter duo was united in changing their life's trajectory.

People might not understand the relationship between a mother and a daughter. The strength of our love, our passion for our tea room business, and our drive to succeed keeps us going – and as long as we have each other – we will keep moving forward! We have a lot in common, we finish each other's sentences, and complete each other's thoughts. We are funny people: we make people laugh, we love to sing, tell stories, act and reenact, and basically just have fun while we do what we love to do.

We love to hear people make yummy noises as they taste our food. We visit each table in the tea room to see how our customers are doing. We offer refills on soup and ensure that no one leaves without a full belly. We recently had a reservation for a family of three women and a man. After a few minutes we learned that the man was named Bruno. The song, "We don't talk about Bruno" from the movie 'Encanto' just came out of our mouths! This is typical for us, since we are a singing family. Luckily the customers found it hilarious, too!

But this book is not about our family, even though our story is based on family and why we opened a tea room. Leila (mother), Erika (daughter), and Shelly (husband and father) make up our little family. We used to have Charlotte, our matriarch, mother and grandmother), three generations of strong women in the business, but she passed away a few years before this book was written. Charlotte sat by the front door of the tea room as a greeter until the day a customer asked her what her favorite flavor of our teas was and she answered, in her distinct New York accent, "I don't drink tea, I like only coffee!" Thinking she was not good for business, Charlie (Charlotte's nickname as we called her) was then banished to the back of the store. She told people she guarded the bathrooms, making sure no one took the extra rolls of toilet paper or paper towels. Charlie was a great influence on our sense of humor.

In the tea room each of us have specific duties, even though we get together to help each other as needed. Erika is on the phone all day and into the wee hours of the night. Customers often call late at night and tell Erika, "I didn't think anyone would answer!" Erika thinks to herself, "Then why did you call?!" They commonly ask her if she is "The Erika" of Erika's Tea Room. We would love to answer "No, duh" but instead we politely assure customers that she is. Erika is also the saleswoman extraordinaire; she spends hours with customers helping them find everything from tea, to tea sets, and their perfect scone bundle gifts.

Leila is the head "Sconista"; well, the only Sconista, really! She spends most of the day baking scones. When we expect tables, she diverts her efforts into making yummy salads, quiche, soups, and desserts. On the days of tea tables, Leila bakes before the tables come in and after they leave. Just like the Post Office motto, 'Through rain or snow or sleet or hail, scones need to be sent and delivered by mail!'

Leila typically comes up with the recipes that go along with Erika's creative menus. For Halloween, Erika added a Pumpkin Spice Scone. Leila thought of all the great spices of the fall season. She used pumpkin spice, cardamon, and cinnamon. But of course, that was not good enough for Leila. She then thought of what chocolates, nuts, or dried fruits would enhance the flavors. With so many to choose from, Leila thought of white chocolate with cranberries, semi-sweet chocolate with pecans, or dark chocolate with hazelnuts. This is a typical process when Leila is coming up with the recipe for one of Erika's menu items. This shows how Erika and Leila are the perfect yin and yang.

Leila has to be able to quickly switch gears in the tea room–from making silk flower centerpieces for each table, to baking, to cooking, to serving, and to helping choose the perfect tea. She puts her heart into everything she does. Her attention to detail is of utmost importance. Leila wants every guest to feel like they are the most important one. It is evident that Erika's heart is also in whatever she does. Erika switches from selling the tea, scones, and tea paraphernalia in the store to selling it all online, and personally on the phone as well. Erika gets so much pleasure from what she does and spends as much time with a customer as they want or need. Leila explains that Erika is so much like her, that sometimes you can't tell the difference between them.

Now let us introduce Shelly. He is the head dishwasher and president of the custodial staff of one. He is the only person in the kitchen who did not get pregnant washing dishes. We hired several other dishwashers. Within six months of washing dishes, they were all pregnant! It had to be something in the water, we said. (Don't worry; the water we use for tea is purified.) Shelly also does all the running of errands such as getting all the shipments mailed and picking up any needed ingredients. If we have any heavy lifting, you would think Shelly would handle it, but typically Erika does. As we always say, Shelly is too light for heavy work and too heavy for light work.

We cannot leave out the most important person in our introduction, Charlie. Charlotte taught Leila how to cook. She was the first instinctual cook. That means she did not follow recipes, she made it up as she cooked (a pinch of this, a dash of that, a tad of something else). Nothing was ever written down, but at the young age of six, Leila would help her mom in the kitchen preparing meals. Leila always wished Erika would follow in her footsteps, but Erika always wanted to be management instead. The only thing that Charlie couldn't do was bake. She could not bake at all. If the recipe called for a teaspoon of lemon juice, Charlie would use a cup full. She knew that lemon is delicious in sponge cake, so the more the better, she thought! We joked that the garbage man got a hernia picking up the sponge cake we had to throw out.

Customers often ask us why we named the business Erika's Tea Room. Part of the Jewish heritage is the belief that everything is "Beshert", translated as "Meant to Be". Leila wanted the name to be Erika's Tea Room right from the start. She believed that all her luck and happiness in the world begins and ends with Erika. Erika was still unsure and tossed around a few other names. Then one day the corporation papers came back from the State of Florida and they were filed and stamped with January 24th on them. This is Erika's birthdate. See, it was "Beshert"!

Now that we have introduced the main characters of our story, we are eager to share some great tea room recipes along with the stories behind them with you!

THE NEED TO FEED

Many people enter our doors and ask, "Are you a real tearoom?" We reply, "We tried being a fake one, but it just didn't work!" "Tea" is not only our passion, it is our life, love, and career. We have been going to tea rooms for years. Going to tea rooms was a special 'Mommy and Me' tradition that we started a long time ago and continue as we travel today. Let me paint a picture of an adorable little girl with bright blue eyes, blond pigtails, and deep dimples holding her first China teacup. Ahhh, the memories we have created over tea! That is why we created our slogan, "Memories Made with Every Cup."

The "Need to Feed" was Charlie's way of doing things that was handed down from generation to generation. When Leila was a young girl, she learned to cook at her mother's side. Charlie fed anyone who entered her home, regardless of the time of day. Leila has the same reputation. Nieces, nephews, family, and friends entered and, almost immediately, whatever was in the fridge was put together for a hot meal. Leila hoped that Erika would follow the tradition. In present day, when Erika is asked by customers if she does any of the food preparation, she replies, "I do not have time, I am management. Someone needs to keep Leila on task and crack the whip."

In this tradition, we aim to feed all of our customers with filling sandwiches and quiches as well as a daily homemade soup. We are known for our wonderful, healthy soups and typically offer a complimentary refill. The offer of more soup came from Leila's childhood. We were once invited to Aunt Betty's house for

Passover dinner. It was the first time that the kids were allowed to have a taste of Manischewitz grape wine, and Leila's sister polished off all of the kids' wine. When the soup finally came to the kids, there was a big matzo ball in the middle of the bowl and just a small spoonful of soup. Being a little drunk, Leila's sister started to cry. When asked why, she retorted that the big thing in the middle of her bowl ate up all the soup! And so the tradition of always offering more soup started. Leila did not want anyone to leave the tearoom hungry.

Before we opened the tearoom, Erika had a funny soup adventure as well. She was seriously dating a young man from Missouri, and one Passover she went home with him for dinner. His mom made chicken soup. Before serving, she asked Erika if she liked carrots, and then proceeded to give Erika the one baby carrot that she had put in the soup! Needless to say, everyone else had a bowl of plain broth. Erika couldn't wait to tell her mom because all of Leila's family loved the vegetables she put into her chicken soup. She put several whole onions, a bag of baby carrots, multiple cut up celery stalks, parsnips, turnips, and fresh parsley and dill in her homemade chicken stock. Of course, chicken cutlets were also added since Leila's soup can be a meal in itself. There was no fighting over the veggies this time–there was plenty for all!

Instead of chicken soup (although you can guess the recipe based on our previous story!) we want to share a soup that was literally Charlie's favorite meal: Unstuffed Cabbage Soup. Charlie loved stuffed cabbage. This came down from our Polish roots. Charlie always used to put raisins and rice into the meat and sliced apples into the sauce to make it sweet. Also, some sour salt and sugar was added to the tomato sauce. Leila says that this was one of Charlie's signature dishes. To make it her own, Leila took stuffed cabbage and made it into a crowd-pleasing soup. Charlie used ground beef and fresh cabbage and cooked it until it was soft, usually a whole day at a low temperature. Leila figured out a way to make the same great taste for less cooking time and with healthier ingredients using ground turkey for the meatballs and baking them until fully cooked. She used tomato juice as the base of her soup that already has a sourish undertone. Instead of the apples and all that sugar, Leila used apple sauce and less sugar. She boiled the cabbage until soft and then assembled her soup. Unstuffed cabbage soup became one of Leila's signature soups in her continued "Need to Feed" venture.

Unstuffed Cabbage Soup

INGREDIENTS

1 small green cabbage

1 pound package 93%-lean ground turkey

¼ cup cooked brown rice

¼ cup raisins

2 Tablespoons minced onions

1 teaspoon garlic powder

1 teaspoon ground onion powder

1 teaspoon ground black pepper

2 large eggs

1 cup of flavored breadcrumbs

½ cup sugar

1 64-ounce or 2 32-ounce tomato juice

1 small jar applesauce

DIRECTIONS

1. Preheat the oven to 375 degrees F.

2. Boil cabbage in salted water until fork-tender and then chop.

3. In a large bowl mix the turkey, spices, and eggs until well blended. Add rice and raisins. Add breadcrumbs.

4. Spray a lasagna pan (it can be a disposable one) with baking spray. Form meatballs and bake for 30 minutes or until meatballs are brown.

5. When the meatballs are fully cooked, cut them into quarters.

6. To assemble the soup, pour tomato juice in first, add meatballs, cabbage, and applesauce.

7. Bring to a boil, then put the soup on low, add sugar, and cook until you are ready to serve.

Leila's Tasteful Tips

- You can use white or other rice as desired.

- If you are diabetic or watching your sugar, substitute sugar-free applesauce and use your favorite sugar substitute such as stevia in the raw.

- If you are a vegetarian, leave the meatballs out and replace with 2 12-ounce bags of frozen carrots.

- You can also substitute cranberries for the raisins. This makes great porcupine meatballs that make very tasty hot appetizers.

The Need to Feed continues with our motto: "People enter as strangers but leave as friends." We have many customers that come to us to celebrate their birthdays. When we opened the tearoom, we used to sing the Happy Birthday song to our birthday pals. One day, a customer told us this was not legal, so we wrote our own song to the tune of "I'm a Little Teapot". We sing, "We're a little tea room, cute and sweet. For your birthday here's a treat. To celebrate your birthday is the thing, so Happy Birthday, we all sing!" Just like we do when we travel, we wanted our tea room to be our customer's celebration place.

By visiting other tea rooms, we learned early on that the most memorable tea rooms served homemade salads, scones, soups, and desserts. While talking about opening the tea room, Leila told Erika that she would only use the best real-food ingredients. Whenever we think about chicken out of a can, Leila cringes. How do they get chicken into the can to begin with? Leila makes enough food for the amount of people coming in on any specific day. So, it's always fresh, never frozen.

To this day, Leila remembers a childhood story about her Uncle Abe. Uncle Abe owned a neighborhood luncheonette. Today it would be called a café or deli. Back then, there weren't individual tables. Instead, there was a huge counter with attached bar stools. Abe's wife, Aunt Betty, made the best malteds and egg creams and Uncle Abe made the sandwiches. As a child of the depression era, Uncle Abe refused to buy fresh luncheon meats until the old meats were totally sold out. One day, a young man ordered a ham and cheese sandwich with mayonnaise. Uncle Abe served it promptly with a handful of broken potato chips. The man turned to Abe and asked him why the ham was green. Uncle Abe retorted emphatically, "Oh, I am sorry, I served you the imported ham by mistake. That is usually a more expensive sandwich, but because this was my mistake, I won't charge you more." The funny part of this story is that the young man came back a week later for more of the imported ham. You thought that Dr. Seuss came up with the concept of "Green Eggs and Ham", but he must have borrowed it from Uncle Abe!

Having a baby or bridal shower has been linked with the English High Tea experience. Erika sits down with all the shower planners and helps them personalize their special High Tea menu. She assists with all aspects of the party from tea selections to custom desserts, and then Leila creates the recipes. Even though the menu is created especially for each event, Leila always prepares for the unexpected. It is usually the unexpected gluten-free or vegetarian plate that needs attention. The latest bridal shower threw Leila a curveball. The bride and an additional attendee had gone through bariatric surgery, so it was a good thing that Leila made a vat of tomato bisque soup. Seconds and a few thirds of the soup was a crowd pleaser. The lettuce garnish became a good base for the chicken salad made for the sandwiches. Everyone was sated, which satisfied Leila's "Need to Feed".

A customer once came in and selected one of our tuna sandwiches, but she sent the sandwich back, stating that it was fishy. We replied that tuna is a fish. She exclaimed, "It is?!" She never thought tuna was a fish! Leila also loves to have everyone sit and have lunch together. Our tea barista joins our family at the middle table every day for lunch. Seeing Leila starting to set the middle table for lunch, a customer once confronted her. "Isn't it great that Erika allows you to have lunch here?" Leila retorted, "Not only does she allow me to have lunch, she allows me to make it as well!"

When Leila was a young teenager, she worked upstate New York in a Catskills hotel. She was the arts and crafts counselor from the time she was fourteen until around eighteen. All the counselors watched the kids from breakfast until 4 PM and then again from 5 PM until midnight. On her hour break, Leila went into the kitchen to watch what the cooks were making for dinner. On Shabbat, Friday evenings and Saturdays until sundown, the cooks could not turn on the ovens or stoves. It was typical to make cold soups on these days. It was not uncommon to have cold borscht (beet soup), cold potato soup, and cold cucumber soup. Leila's favorites were the cold fruit soups, such as strawberry soup, watermelon soup, or peach soup, to name just a few. Most of our Mother's Day special menus include one of these cold soups that garner attendee accolades. Leila just happened to make a cold peach soup at one of our guest's requests, so let us share the simple recipe with you.

Chilled Peach Soup Recipe

INGREDIENTS

2 15-ounce cans of sliced peaches in heavy syrup

1 16-ounce sour cream

1 32-ounce heavy cream

¼ cup granulated sugar

DIRECTIONS

1. Put both cans of peaches with all the juice in a gallon pitcher.
2. Using an immersion blender, crush the peaches.
3. Add the sour cream and the sugar (continue to combine with the immersion blender).
4. Add the heavy cream (continue to combine with the immersion blender).
5. Chill overnight and stir before serving.

Leila's Tasteful Tips

- Take a fresh peach, cut it in half, and make thin slices for soup garnish.
- Instead of peaches, use a 16-ounce bag of frozen fruits (mango, strawberries, blueberries, cherries). Instead of ¼ cup of sugar, use ½ cup.
- If you prefer, garnish with a fresh mint leaf or a dollop of sour cream.

When it comes to food, Charlie would eat, but not much! When Leila would cook for her, she did a little bit better. As Charlie got older, she did not eat food with much gusto. A fond memory of her was when we visited the pecan store in Georgia. Charlie loved her chocolate-covered nut samples. She could not make up her mind about which chocolate she liked more. Charlie tasted white chocolate, dark chocolate, milk chocolate, coffee dusted, powdered sugar and many more until her face was covered in chocolate! To make sure she ate something during the day (other than chocolate-coated nuts!),Leila made Charlie a scone and a cup of hot chocolate. Her eyes would light up, and it was their time during the day when Leila and Charlie could sit down to have a talk. These memories are bittersweet. We think of and miss Charlie daily.

Leila was once in the kitchen cutting up some fresh mangoes to take home. Erika came in and started sampling the mangoes already sliced and stated, "These four mangoes did not make much!" Leila replied, "They made much more before you ate them!" Erika laughed as she grabbed one more mango slice before packing them up to take home. This reminded Leila about a time before Erika was born. Leila was babysitting her nephew and had just bought him an Easy-Bake Oven. She helped her nephew stir the water into the cake mixes to bake two cakes, one vanilla and one chocolate. They pushed the cake pans into the oven and waited for the appropriate time. Leila told her nephew that he could choose one to eat and then to put one aside to take home to feed his mother. You have to understand that the cake was a big 2 inches wide by 1 inch high. As Leila was cleaning the pans to put away, she noticed that her nephew had eaten both cakes. Leila guessed he hadn't acquired the family "Need to Feed" obsession!

In the tea room, Leila's "Need to Feed" obsession continues with every guest who enters. She is not satisfied until she hears every guest say that they have full bellies and that they enjoyed all that was eaten. When Erika was a little girl, Leila asked her, "Do you want a fat mommy or a skinny mommy?" Erika innocently asked her mother, "What is the difference?" Leila then explained, "A skinny mommy says, 'I'm sorry you are having a bad day. Let's eat some tofu and then jog around the block.' Whereas a fat mommy gives her sweet daughter a wet kiss and states, 'Why don't we bake some chocolate chip cookies, make a pot of tea, and veg in front of the tv?'" Leila then asked Erika which one she would prefer. No surprise which mommy she chose!

VISITING OTHER TEAROOMS

The High Tea Experience makes any occasion special. What is served and how it is served and the beautiful atmosphere it is served in is what makes the experience memorable. Even though what we do in the tea room is really not a real High Tea, it has become the common name for what we offer. As Americans, the tradition of tea, petite foods, and desserts or sweets is best known as a High Tea. We enjoy watching how each individual tea room makes the High Tea experience their own.

Over the course of years, we have visited over fifty different tea rooms. Every year we would make many special birthday reservations and seek out tea rooms when we traveled near and far. It is intriguing how different each tea room was. Some used multi-tiered servers and others served in courses. We decided what our favorite features were and adjusted our service accordingly. We made it a ritual to select the same item to taste first so that we could compare thoughts quietly. If Erika jumped ahead or didn't choose the same item, a quick hand smack kept her on task. Of course, the scone came first, and we chatted secretly as we ate each sweet bite. But first we smothered each piece with delectable Clotted cream or Devonshire cream and either preserves or lemon curd. Our favorite is always strawberry. Most tea rooms we visited made plain, cranberry, or blueberry scones. Then we searched our three-tiered serving tray for the savory or sandwich that we would each take. We talked about the taste as if we were food critics. We didn't know what we liked better. One tea room served their treats on white paper doilies placed strategically on a cream colored unfolded three tier server and another had beautiful China on metal three-tiered holders. It is very exciting to see the differences and similarities in each tea room. Some cut each sandwich into shapes, while others made careful tiers, and still others created miniature buns or mini croissants. Although we always see the tea room owner's unique spin on the High Tea experience, the commonalities keep customers coming back for more.

The very first tea room we visited was on a family vacation in Florida. We had no idea that this visit would someday influence our decision to open a tea room so many years later. It is funny that our story begins and is currently in Florida! So, our story is coming full circle. The tearoom in Florida set up an elegant tea parlor, with white-glove service. Their cucumber sandwiches, which they made open-faced, quickly became a staple for us. Customers cry if we do not have cucumber sandwiches to serve!

When we take reservations, customers put in their requests. Cucumber sandwiches are just one of our many customer favorites. In later chapters we will share more of our fan favorites, such as scone choices, soups, and sandwiches that our guests keep coming back for. Customers often ask Erika if they can take Leila home to cook and bake for them. Erika tries to sell Leila (or at least her cooking and baking skills) to the highest bidder – which fits into Erika's need to sell anything that's not nailed down!

Cucumber Sandwich Recipe

INGREDIENTS

8-ounce whipped cream cheese

2 Tablespoons dried chives

1 teaspoon of each onion powder, garlic powder, and ground black pepper

1 English cucumber (peeled)

1 loaf of Cuban bread, sliced

DIRECTIONS

1. With a spoon, mix cream cheese and spices. Set aside.

2. Using a mandolin, thinly slice the cucumber.

3. Put a thin smear of the chive cream cheese on two slices of bread.

4. Put 5 to 6 slices of cucumber to assemble a sandwich.

Leila's Tasteful Tips

- Instead of dried chives, substitute dried dill.

- Instead of Cuban bread, use your favorite white or wheat bread. Cut off all the edges. You can cut the bread into triangles or other shapes, or make a three-tiered sandwich. Make sure to smear each slice with the cream cheese mixture.

- Gluten-free or carb-free options – Cut a thicker slice of the cucumber and smear the cream cheese directly on top of it. To peel or not to peel, that is the question! It is up to you whether or not you peel the cucumber. We believe, peel.

loser to home in New Jersey, we found a tea room that became our local go-to spot. The owner served delicious scones, chicken salad, and onion tartlets. This tea room was in an old Victorian home. They had a nice size retail space as you walked in and sold everything from loose leaf tea to teapots and other tea essentials. We learned so much from this tea room. We knew that we wanted to make salads with real ingredients (fresh chicken or turkey), not ingredients out of a can. Their onion tartlets were irresistible, but where their tartlets were a pop-in-your-mouth treat, we decided to go big or go home. We added a choice of a full slice of quiche to our tea plate.

We introduced our different quiches to rave reviews. We make quiches with a crust and also a crustless version. We do gluten-free quiche upon request. Leila's quiches are packed with veggies, bacon, cheese…Oh my! Leila's creativity is endless. One of our High Tea options comes with a slice of quiche and a tea sandwich plus soup. After trying a slice of quiche, we have many customers ordering a whole quiche to take home. They can never get enough. Trying to settle on just one quiche favorite is not easy. We never know if it is the broccoli bacon or quiche Lorraine that is the number-one seller. The fav seems to change daily!

What's better than one scone? A basket of scones!

Quiche Lorraine Frittata Recipe

INGREDIENTS

1 12-ounce steamable frozen chopped spinach (microwave for 5-6 minutes)

1/2 cup fully cooked lean real bacon bits (I use Hormel 40% lean real bacon bits)

10 large eggs

1 pint of half-and-half or heavy cream

1 teaspoon of each garlic powder, onion powder, and ground pepper

1 cup shredded Swiss cheese (or 1 8-ounce package)

½ cup Bisquick baking mix

DIRECTIONS

1. Preheat the oven to 375 degrees F.

2. Steam frozen spinach for 6 minutes. Open the package on paper towels to get rid of any excess moisture, and then set aside to cool.

3. Whisk eggs, half-and-half, and spices until fluffy.

4. Add Bisquick and whisk until mixture is well blended.

5. Mix the spinach, bacon, and cheese together and spread evenly on the bottom of a disposable 9x11 pan.

6. Pour egg mixture over spinach mixture.

7. Bake for 35 to 40 minutes or until golden brown.

Leila's Tasty Tips

- You can substitute fully cooked turkey bacon – follow the directions on the box and crumble before adding.
- You can substitute broccoli for spinach (or use asparagus).
- You can change the cheese to cheddar for another great taste.
- You can also add ¼ of a cup of dried chives.

In Quebec, Canada, we visited a tea room that was in an old hotel. They had custom-made China, very Alice-in-Wonderland like, and beautiful three-tiered servers. The whole High Tea was presented on the server. Their sandwiches were so pretty, we hesitated to eat them. They made tartlet cups that housed their salads. Fresh smoked salmon was on an open-faced bread and then a mini-bun had duck confit nestling on it. When we took the idea of these delights back to our kitchen, we took the duck confit concept to create a miniature Cornish pastie. A Cornish pastie is very English. Instead of duck, we used chicken as the filling, with caramelized onions chopped finely. Both renditions were very tasty. Our reboot recipes became a way for us to demonstrate our take on something we had enjoyed at another tea room. As Laverne and Shirley once said, "We do it our way, just our way!"

Cornish Pastie Recipe

DOUGH INGREDIENTS

2 cups all-purpose flour and a bit
more to roll out the dough
½ teaspoon salt
½ cup shortening
½ cup cold water
1 teaspoon of each onion powder,
garlic powder, and pepper

TO BRUSH PASTIE

1 beaten egg with ¼ cup water

FILLING INGREDIENTS

1 medium chicken breast
1 Tablespoon all-purpose flour
1 16-ounce low-sodium chicken stock
2 Tablespoons canola oil
1 medium sweet onion (peeled and
chopped)
1 teaspoon of each onion powder,
garlic powder, and pepper
¼ cup canned carrots (smashed)

DIRECTIONS

1. Preheat the oven to 350 degrees F.

2. To make the dough – mix salt and spices into the flour. Using a pastry blender, cut in shortening until crumbly. Add water a little at a time until a dough ball forms. Cover with a towel and set aside.

3. Cook the chicken cutlet in the stock until fork-soft (you can make it the night before to cool.)

4. Grind the chicken in a small food processor (or you can just pull the chicken apart into small pieces).

5. In a frying pan, caramelize the onion until brown.

6. Mix chicken, carrots, onions, and spices. Add the flour.

7. Flour the parchment paper and roll out the dough to 1/8-inch thickness.

8. Cut the dough with a three-inch biscuit cutter.

9. Put a teaspoon of chicken mixture on one side of each of the dough pieces.

10. Fold the dough in half and crimp the edges closed.

11. Place on a parchment-lined cookie sheet.

12. Prick the top of each pastie with a fork. Brush with the egg mixture.

13. Bake for 20 to 30 minutes or until browned.

Leila's Tasteful Tips

- You can use a can of premade biscuits as a quick pastie dough.
- You can substitute a turkey loin or beef cubes for the chicken.
- You could use fresh or frozen carrots (just put into the stock with the chicken).
- For vegetarians, you could make the pasties filled with potato, caramelized onions, and carrots.

We visited a tea room in South Carolina which was a remodeled firehouse. Since it was built in 1911, there were no elevators in this three-storey building. Erika pushed as Leila pulled Charlie up the three flights of stairs to the tea room. As soon as we reached the table, Charlie said she needed to use the facilities, which were back down on the first floor. We thought about strapping Charlie to the fireman's pole, but it wouldn't have helped get her back up. We asked Charlie why she hadn't gone when we arrived, and she replied: "I can't go on demand!" After we were sure that Charlie was good to go, we sat down at our table on the third floor and the tea hostess gave each of us a glass of peach iced tea. Uh-oh! We were all worried that Charlie would need to go back down the three floors! But luckily she managed to make it through the courses. We were asked to choose our hot tea for the table. Our first course, a blueberry scone with small bowls of their Devon Cream and lemon curd, was served next.

Looking down in the opening in the center of the tearoom you could see down to the first floor and the preparation area. We saw the staff preparing the sandwiches for our tea service. They were cutting the edges off the breads used. They served a chicken salad on wholewheat bread, pimento cheese on cinnamon raisin bread, and a tomato pie pinwheel. This was the first time we saw soup served in small glass tea cups. This inspired us to do the same. We loved that you could see all the ingredients in the soup that was being served.

They had used a scone mix to make their scones and also sold the mix in their retail store. This tea room served their High Tea in multiple courses that were sent up to the third floor on a dumbwaiter. Have you ever wondered how dumbwaiters got their unique name? It is a storage lift used to transport food in restaurants, without noise or odor, not to be confused with a dumb waiter that has to do with intelligence!

Another tea room we visited in Georgia had a Southern flair. They served fried green tomatoes with a dollop of pimento cheese on top. Instead of scones, they had homestyle blueberry pastries. They were delicious. Their High Tea was really different and unique. We couldn't wait to get back to our kitchen to reboot the fried green tomato sampling. We created a baked green tomato with pimento cheese sandwich. The tartness of the green tomato with the cheesy goodness of the pimento cheese is a match made in sandwich heaven.

Green Tomato and Pimento Cheese Sandwich Recipe

INGREDIENTS - PIMENTO CHEESE

8-ounce whipped cream cheese

2 Tablespoons dried chives

1 teaspoon of each onion powder, garlic powder, and ground black pepper

2 Tablespoons diced red pimentos

½ cup mild cheddar cheese

INGREDIENTS - BAKED GREEN TOMATO

1 to 2 green tomatoes (washed, dried, and sliced thinly)

¼ cup olive oil

1 teaspoon of each onion powder, garlic powder, and ground black pepper

1 multigrain loaf of bread, sliced

DIRECTIONS

1. Preheat the oven to 375 degrees F.
2. Place thinly sliced green tomatoes on a parchment-lined cookie sheet.
3. Mix the spices into oil and brush the tomatoes on both sides.
4. Bake the tomatoes for 15 to 20 minutes, or until soft. Then set aside to cool.
5. With a spoon, mix cream cheese and spices. Add pimentos. Add cheddar cheese. Set aside.
6. Cut the ends off the multigrain bread.
7. Put a thin smear of the pimento cheese on two slices of bread.
8. Put a slice or two of the green tomatoes on the bread to assemble a sandwich.

Leila's Tasteful Tips

- You can toast the bread to give the sandwich a nice crunch.
- If you do not care for the tartness of a green tomato, a red one can be substituted.
- Another great alternative is a thin slice of zucchini. Cook the zucchini the same way you would cook the tomato.

We recently visited another tea room in Georgia. They served an "Afternoon Tea Experience" in a beautiful Victorian home. Each table had lace tablecloths, matching water glasses, and two-tier servers. They served their treats on cream and gold charger plates, with individual tea and toast sets. The tea hostess brought out our ginger peach tea which she perched on a tea warmer. The sandwiches had very cute names which included a Ribbon Tea Sandwich and a Mayflower Tea Sandwich. The Ribbon Tea Sandwich consisted of a thin slice of ham with egg salad and the Mayflower Tea Sandwich was a round, pressed white bread made into a calla lily with a smear of cream cheese, orange marmalade, and an almond sliver. It was so pretty to see and even better to eat. If we would do a reboot, it would be our rendition of the Ribbon Tea Sandwich. We would put chopped ham or bacon into the egg salad, but we thoroughly enjoyed their rendition as well. We had a lot in common with the tea room's owners who were also a mother and daughter duo. Nice conversation and great food!

We can't wait until our next excursion, so that we can find another tea room to try. We love to see all the personal touches on a High Tea. The biggest question that arises from all tea rooms is "Crust or No Crust?" when it comes to tea sandwiches. It is definitely more traditional to make small, crustless sandwiches, but we have homemade small breads baked for us, and these lend themselves to leaving the crust on, which is so tasty. Just another example of doing it our way!

Today, we make memories in our own tea room. We take the best of every experience we have encountered in all the tea rooms we visit and bring it back home to our kitchen. We love to help customers cultivate their passion for tea and give them an opportunity to experience various tea room delicacies such as homemade scones, salads, quiche, soups, and desserts. We have always wanted to set up an experience that was not just your grandmother's tea party, doing things that are outside the norm. Our greatest claim to fame is getting each guest to try one of our over one hundred teas and getting them hooked on drinking tea!

THERE'S ALWAYS TIME FOR TEA

Tea is our bag, no pun intended. When Leila was young, she watched an advertisement for Tiny Little Tea Leaves from a brand of tea. Whenever she was sick, Charlie would force her to drink this bitter tea with some honey in it. When Leila's dad was sick, the hot tea had some liquor in it, usually Cherry Herring. Either way, it was not Leila's cup of tea. Leila, being the youngest of three children, was never offered liquor in her tea. She was always treated like a baby and was never old enough to drink. That is why Erika was never offered liquor in her tea. Leila tells her that our tea can stand on its own, never needing any additives. . .

There are a few customers that come to the tea room and say that they do not like tea. We tell them to try one of our teas and assure them that we have a flavor that they will enjoy. We explain that the teas we carry are specially blended and that we have many different types. We talk about the difference between quality tea that is First Flush loose leaf and make a comparison to First Flush wines. We then assist the customer in choosing one of our wonderful blends and typically we can change their opinion on drinking tea!

When we were planning to open the tea room, we decided to learn all we could about tea from one of the most well-known tea experts. He travels throughout the world touring tea plantations in China, Japan, India, Sri Lanka, and Africa. In each of these countries he saw how the tea was harvested and tasted all their delicate leaves in their purest form. When we sat through his classes, we tasted all the basic tea groups. The maestro did not allow us to add sweetener, nor cream. We definitely learned to appreciate the earthiness of each of the distinct flavors of tea.

Then we searched for the top tea blenders in the United States. For every one tea we add to our menu, we discard ten. At any given time, we have over one hundred different tea blends and custom blended flavors. Tea needs a good foundation, like life. Something strong you can always count on. Something familiar you can always come home to. We have tried many teas, in many tea rooms, and the tea makes or breaks a tea room.

We grew up in a coffee environment, which is now a taboo word in the tea room. Tea was not offered in the break rooms at work. Erika and Leila learned about the differences and similarities of the four main tea groups and herbal teas. Tea opened our eyes to new tastes and quickly took over as our daily cuppa. People come in and ask if we have tea from England. We tell them that there aren't actually any tea gardens in England. In fact, English Breakfast tea is grown and harvested in China. They also ask for the famous teas known as "Lip-tone" or "Twin-ings". We joke about the mispronunciation, but these teas were also the only ones we knew growing up. Until we started going to tea rooms, when Erika was much younger, we did not get to taste finer teas. After one taste, we were hooked.

Even though we both have our favorite flavors, we still love to try new special blends. There are tea rooms with just a few selections of tea and others with many. To us, the most important factor is taste. Good, First Flush tea is the ticket. Flushes of tea have to do with the tea plucking times also known as harvests. The reason why first flush tea is the most desired by tea connoisseurs is because of the tea's freshness and delicacy. We learned to appreciate the best First Flush tea leaves that make the most flavorful brews. Our tea barista makes a special pot of First Flush tea for us every afternoon after the tables have left. We love our Velvet Tea. It is a chamomile, peppermint and vanilla blend that is as smooth as its name.

We also experiment with cooking and baking with tea to create new and exciting recipes. Here is a family recipe for Honey Cake improved by exchanging a strong cup of brewed tea for the typical cup of brewed coffee. The improvement on taste is remarkable. Honey Cake was a staple family tradition during our Jewish New Year celebration. On Rosh Hashanah, you eat sweets made with honey to bring in a good, healthy, and sweet New Year to come. It was a tradition to have a piece of Honey Cake for dessert at a Rosh Hashanah dinner. Since Charlie couldn't bake, her Honey Cake came from the local supermarket. Try this recipe for a tasty homemade alternative to store bought.

Leila and Erika's daily cuppa tea always includes a scone!

Honey Cake Recipe

DRY INGREDIENTS

3 ½ cups all-purpose flour

1 Tablespoon baking powder

1 teaspoon baking soda

½ teaspoon salt

2 Tablespoons cinnamon

1 teaspoon cardamom

1 teaspoon allspice

1 ½ cups granulated sugar

½ cup brown sugar

WET INGREDIENTS

3 large eggs

1 cup vegetable oil

1 cup orange blossom honey

1 cup strong brewed tea

½ cup orange juice

DIRECTIONS

1. Preheat the oven to 350 degrees F.
2. Spray a bundt pan with baking spray.
3. Make a strong cup of tea (we use orange and spice tea).
4. In a large bowl, mix all the dry ingredients together.
5. In a second large bowl, whisk the wet ingredients together.
6. With a hand mixer, add the wet ingredients to the dry ingredients.
7. Fill the bundt pan halfway.
8. Bake for 35 to 40 minutes or until a cake tester comes out dry.

Leila's Tasteful Tips

- This cake can take the place of a holiday fruit cake, just add ½ cup fruit cake candied pieces and change the tea to bourbon tea.
- You can add ½ cup cranberries, apricots, or your favorite dried fruit.
- You can add ½ cup walnuts or pecans.

Sometimes the tea pairing is as important as the tea itself. This raises a very important question from tea connoisseurs all over the world: "To dunk or not to dunk, that is the question! Our tea biscuits hold up either way! They can stand on their own two feet. A tea biscuit looks like a biscotti but is much softer and more buttery. We make various flavors of tea biscuits for dessert. Erika's favorite tea biscuit is a white chocolate cranberry, whereas Leila's is a cinnamon semi-sweet chocolate pecan. We also make coconut, fruit cake, and apricot walnut tea biscuits, to name just a few. It is a very easy recipe, and they last in a covered plastic container for two weeks on the counter. Customers underestimate the great taste of a tea biscuit, but once they try it, they are addicted.

Our scones and specially blended tea, made with
the freshest ingredients and of course LOVE!

White Chocolate Cranberry Tea Biscuits Recipe

INGREDIENTS

1 cup butter (2 sticks, melted and cooled)

3 eggs

1 cup granulated sugar

2 teaspoons baking powder

1 cup dried cranberries

½ cup white chocolate chips

3 cups all-purpose flour

DIRECTIONS

1. Preheat the oven to 375 degrees F.
2. Line two cookie sheets with parchment paper.
3. In a large bowl, using a hand mixer, beat the butter, sugar, and eggs.
4. In a second bowl, mix the flour and the baking powder.
5. Using a large spoon, fold the flour mixture into the wet mixture.
6. Fold in the white chocolate chips and cranberries.
7. Form into two loaves, each about 1-inch thick.
8. Bake for 20 minutes or until golden brown.
9. As soon as you take the loaves out of the oven, cut 1-inch slices.
10. Return to the oven for 5 additional minutes.

Leila's Tasteful Tips

- You can add nuts – pecans, macadamia, walnuts, or almonds.
- You can change cranberries for dried blueberries, cherries, or pineapple.
- You can change white chocolate for semi-sweet or milk chocolate chips.

Even though Leila is the majority owner of Erika's Tea Room, customers tell Erika how kind she is to let her mother work for her. Erika adds, "Leila will always have a job at Erika's. It's job security for life!" Customers love to tell us all their woes. We call it "Tea and Therapy." Leila tells Erika that she thinks tea helps people lose their inhibitions, but Erika says that she is not Dear Abbie! We don't understand why tea helps people to spill their guts. Maybe tea is some kind of lubricant. We learn about customer's mother-in-law issues, husband issues, and/or health issues. Is it loose leaf tea or loose *lip* tea? We think both!

SCONES

Using the finest ingredients (chocolates, nuts, fruits, spices, extracts), Leila, the head Sconista, has created the freshest, flakiest, most decadent scones you have ever tasted. With over thirty varieties now developed, there is definitely a flavor for everyone's taste. In addition to our most popular flavors, we also create seasonal favorites. All of our flavors are available in regular or gluten-free varieties. When Leila is adding ingredients to her scones, she always looks to see if there is enough fruit, enough nuts, or enough chocolate in the mixture, and then adds some more for good measure. Leila feels that if it is a blueberry white-chocolate scone there better be blueberries and white chocolate in every bite! We do not want the flavor on the top of the scone, we want the flavor to be throughout.

Just like Popeye eats spinach to get muscles, Leila rolls out the scone dough. You should see her muscles! Our scones are made daily from scratch by our Head Sconista. We play with scone flavors continuously, making every scone with love. After years of discovery, trying to create different base recipes in Erika's Tea Room kitchen, Leila has developed her own perfect secret base formula for her tea room scones using the very best ingredients.

There are many toppings that are used to enhance the scone experience. Various jams or jellies, as well as lemon curd, are used most frequently. A lot of people like to warm their scone and slather it with butter. The most fabulous topping for a scone is Devon Cream or Clotted Cream. This delectable topping is second cousin to whipped cream and definitely enriches the scone without taking away from the scone's flavor. A frequently asked scone question is why do we make Devon Cream as an alternative to clotted cream?

In England, clotted cream comes from the counties of Devon and Cornwall, where it is made by heating full-fat cow's milk until it clots or the cream rises to the surface. The climate in Florida does not allow cream to clot. Our milk fat is not as thick. Leila would advise you not to buy any of the clotted creams that come in jars. Yuk! It does not taste like the cream from England. Devonshire Cream (abbreviated to Devon Cream) was introduced in the county of Devon, England, using milk from Devon cows. Erika tells everyone that Leila is mean and would not buy her a Devon cow and that is why we have to make a mock Devon Cream in the tea room. Leila's white chocolate Devon Cream is another crowd pleaser and many lick the bowl! What comes first, the cream or the jam? In Devon, cream is traditionally spread first and then topped with jam. In Cornwall, it's the opposite: jam first, then cream. But at the end of the day, smear the scone with both, as you like it, and enjoy.

Which comes first: the chicken or the egg? In the tea world, we often ask the question, which comes first: the actual tea or the tea pairing? This is where our custom tea blending stems from. We start with a good black, white, green, or tisane tea and add cocoa nibs, herbs, dried fruits, spices and/or flowers to create a unique blend. All of our tea blends inspire us to match the tea flavors to the scone flavors. In a few instances we do create a unique scone and then blend the teas to match. We just want to make sure that every pairing is the perfect pairing.

We knew from the start that the scone(s) we served were extremely important to our tea room's success. When we trained at the hand of a Tea Maestro who owned a very successful tea room at one time, he told us that if we made homemade scones each day, we would burn out and it would not be sustainable. One of our business mentors told us that Leila should be replaced and we should hire someone who could bake the scones. There is no one on earth that would put all their heart and soul into each and every scone. We can tell you that our handmade scones have not only kept us going but they have also been instrumental in reaching new customers, and for devoted customers coming back time and time again. A little bit of passion goes a long way!

One day, one of our tearoom customers called Leila over to her table. She was extremely agitated. When Leila asked her what was wrong, she said, "Look at my scone and look at my friend's!" "What am I looking at?" Leila replied, smiling. The customer further explained, "My scone is smaller than my friend's." What Leila wanted to say was that she would take a bite out of her friend's scone to make it equal, but in actuality, Leila explained that the biscuit cutter she used for each scone is the same, but she can't control how high or wide the scone would end up after baking. This is the charm of homemade food – every bite has its own unique personality. We think that in today's world we have become so accustomed to food that looks cookie-cutter identical. Our tearoom is about getting back in touch with the heart of food – slowing down, remembering how to enjoy the simple pleasures of good scones, good food, good tea, and good friends.

Time to bake the scones! Leila is crying in pain after baking for twelve hours straight with no break. Erika is crying, "Why don't we have more orders?!" Our scones are made in small batches, by hand, and from scratch. We vary the flavor of our scones. There are so many flavors to choose from, so why pigeonhole the flavor of our scones? Have you ever read the book, "The Color Kittens"? They loved to paint with all the colors of the world. That is our model for scones. Why not use all the flavors available to us as our palette for making decadent scones? The possibilities are endless!

We love to create opportunities to interact with our customers. Twice a year we run a 'Name the Scone' campaign. If people can name flavors of potato chips, then why not scones? Followers come up with over a hundred new flavors such as blueberry goat's cheese, zucchini walnut, Root beer float, everything bagel, Key lime, dulce de leche, tomato basil, spumoni, strawberry rhubarb, derby, lemon mascarpone, and sweet potato, just to name some winners. Customers would preorder the winning flavors and then vote on their favorite. The person who submitted the scone that received the largest number of votes wins a complimentary box of scones. It is so fun to run this campaign and Leila gets so creative making the scones!

Leila thrives on a challenge. Give her the most out-of-the-ordinary flavor combination and she will rise to the task! Don't think that all the flavors Leila tries work. Once in a while there is a faux pas. Leila tried to make a blueberry blue cheese scone. She loved the blueberry goat cheese and thought this would work as well. Sorry, the blue cheese was extremely off-putting. Leila loves the trial and error (or should we say trial and success) of creating a new scone flavor. For the most part, Leila has not met a scone flavor she did not like.

Blueberry Cream Cheese Scone Recipe

INGREDIENTS

2 1/2 cups all-purpose flour

½ cup sugar

2 teaspoons baking powder

½ teaspoon salt

½ cup or 1 stick cold butter

3 ounces cream cheese

1/3 cup heavy cream

¼ cup dried blueberries

DIRECTIONS

1. Preheat the oven to 375 degrees F.
2. Line a baking sheet with parchment paper.
3. In a medium bowl, combine all the dry ingredients (flour, sugar, salt, baking powder).
4. Using a pastry blender, cut in the butter and cream cheese until the mixture resembles coarse crumbs.
5. Add the heavy cream by using the pastry cutter to combine.
6. Then, using your hands, form a dough ball.
7. Fold in the dried blueberries.
8. On a piece of parchment paper, flour the surface and roll out the dough to ½ inch thickness.
9. Using a biscuit cutter, cut out scones (rerolling dough as needed).
10. Makes approximately 12 scones.
11. Bake until brown, about 12 minutes.

Leila's Tasteful Tips

- Always use cold butter and cream. This makes for a flakier, softer scone.
- When adding your favorite flavor enhancers, always add dry to dry and wet to wet. For example, if you want to add rose petals, dry ginger, spices, etc., you would add this to the flour mixture. In the same way, if you wanted to add almond extract, orange marmalade, a liquor, etc., you would add this to the egg mixture.
- To cut a scone use a three-inch biscuit cutter. Do not turn or twist the cutter or else the scone will not rise to its full height.
- You can substitute other dried fruits (dates, figs, cranberries, etc.).
- You can substitute three ounces of goat cheese in place of the cream cheese.

Mock Devon Cream Recipe

INGREDIENTS

3 ounces of cream cheese

2 Tablespoons confectioners' sugar

1 cup heavy whipping cream

DIRECTIONS

1. In a mixing bowl, combine the cream cheese and the sugar.
2. Using an electric mixer, beat in the heavy cream until your desired thickness.
3. Refrigerate overnight.

Leila's Tasteful Tips

- Use cold heavy cream (it whips faster).
- You can add vanilla or almond extract (1 teaspoon) to the cream cheese and sugar mixture if desired.

B efore Leila decided to use her classic scone recipe, she experimented with different base recipes. She interchanged buttermilk, cream cheese, sour cream, butter, and heavy cream to see which made the softest, flakiest scone. Additionally, she wanted to see which of these ingredients gave the scone the longest shelf life. Our scones do not contain any preservatives. Some of these recipes have eggs in them and others do not. At the time of these experiments, we had friends and co-workers performing the job of taste testers. Leila really had to twist people's arms to taste all the different scones. When asked which scone was their favorite, the answer was always the one they had in their mouths!

In every good story there is always a dream sequence. In this dream sequence, Leila is having a nightmare about thousands of scones on baking trays attacking her while Erika is whispering in her ear, "We need twelve strawberry, thirty-six black currant, twenty-four Crème Brûlée, six toasted coconut, fifty-four lemon blueberry, twelve orange cranberry…" and so on and so on and so on. Wake up, Leila, it's time to make the scones!

Leila wakes up and prepares to venture to her home, her kitchen in Erika's Tea Room, where the magic happens. This is definitely her happy place, where imagination and skill come together to create today's menu of scones. Leila looks at the list Erika has prepared for her. Written in Erika's handwriting is a list of scones Leila has to make. There are twelve strawberry, thirty-six black currant, twenty-four Crème Brûlée , six toasted coconut, fifty-four lemon blueberry, and twelve orange cranberry. Leila looks extremely perplexed and thinks, was that a dream?!

Erika's dream sequence revolves around our scone and gift bundles. She dreams about what tea set she can pair with what scones, what infuser mug or other tea item will go with scones and tea. Erika dreams about how many more scone and gift bundles she can sell before she gets up in the morning. Ah, Nirvana!

Erika wakes up and as she is brushing her teeth the phone rings with the first order of the day. The customer wants to order her newest tea set and scone bundle. Then Erika takes a quick glimpse of her iPhone and notices that another customer has ordered her usual eight dozen scones. She quickly finishes dressing before telling her mom that her list of scones for the day are light by eight and a half dozen! Be careful what you wish for!

We live in an adult community in the State of Florida. For anyone who does not know what that means, it is a gated community for adults over fifty-five years of age. It is already eighty degrees outside, soon going up to the high nineties. We're on the way to the store as we pass a man supposedly walking his dog, or is that role reversed? Erika is driving, as usual, and Leila is directing her driving, until they come to a complete stop. The dog is sitting very properly under a big tree with a big smile on his doggie face. The man is walking back and forth in front of the dog, also with a big smile on his human face. Then the dog gives off a small "Arf!" as if to say, "You take a walk, I'll watch you from under this tree!" Erika smiled at the man, all knowingly, as the man waived. At that moment,

Leila knew exactly what to tell Erika. "You make the scones today, I will be very content sitting under this tree with the doggie!"

Leila wants everyone to know that a scone by any other name is just a biscuit. She feels that the savory scones that people try to make are a poor imitation. Scones need to be sweet to make them the perfect sidekick for tea. Anytime Leila thinks of a cheddar cheese and chive scone, she thinks of a chain fish restaurant that serves cheddar cheese and chive biscuits. What makes a scone is the creamy, buttery taste. Now add fruit, chocolate, and nuts – wow, perfection!

Every day we meet new tea, teapot, and scone lovers who enter the tea room doors. One day, Jean and her sister came to visit the tea room. Jean asked Erika, "What is that heavenly aroma? It smells delicious!" Just at that moment, Leila came out of the kitchen with a tray of freshly baked pumpkin pecan scones. Erika told the sisters from Pennsylvania, "Mom has been baking all morning." Jean responded, "I just want to lick the air!" Leila and Erika looked at each other and then quickly brought the scones back into the kitchen. We didn't want Jean to get any ideas of licking the scones instead of the air. After all, these scones were destined to be shipped to a customer in Oregon.

Erika wants Leila to plan for the next year. She calls it, "A Scone for all Seasons!" January to start the year off right, of course with the right scone. Have a Happy New Year with a strawberry champagne scone. February you're my little Valentine. A chocolate covered cherry scone would be nice. March, I want to march my Bailey's scone down the aisle until St. Paddy's Day is over.

April, you're my Easter bunny and my Carrot Cake scone will make you smile. And so on and so on. . . Fourth of July, like a firecracker; a red, white, and blue scone. October, a Halloween scone such as candy corn. November brings Thanksgiving scones like pumpkin spice. Last but not least, December, the piece de resistance, Christmas scones lend to the most wonderful time of the year, with Candy Cane, Fruit Cake, Eggnog, and Gingerbread scones, just to name a few. We love our little Calendar of Scones – there is one for every day of the year!

Following in the footsteps of tradition, Leila makes scones with all her heart and soul. While scones have always been a part of the tea experience, Leila wants everyone to taste the love that goes into every bite. She says, "It is more than throwing ingredients into a bowl that makes an Erika's Tea Room scone. It's the hands in the dough that assures the consistency is just right and the keen eyes that makes sure all the flavors are just so!" You are not going to get scones like these anywhere else. From Erika's Tea Room kitchen to yours, our scones are sent to you with love.

Some walk 500 miles... We buy 500 tea sets!

Cinnamon Toffee Scones

INGREDIENTS

2 cups all-purpose flour

1/3 cup granulated sugar

2 teaspoons baking powder

2 teaspoons cinnamon

¼ teaspoon salt

3 Tablespoons unsalted butter

½ cup sour cream

1 large egg

1/3 cup milk chocolate toffee bits

DIRECTIONS

1. Preheat the oven to 375 degrees F.
2. Line a baking sheet with parchment paper.
3. In a large bowl, using a pastry cutter, combine all the dry ingredients (flour, sugar, cinnamon, salt, baking powder).
4. Cut in the cold butter.
5. Whisk the sour cream and egg.
6. Cut into the dry mixture.
7. Using your hands, add toffee bits and form balls.
8. Sprinkle some flour on a parchment sheet.
9. Roll out the dough to ½ inch thickness.
10. Using a three-inch biscuit cutter, cut out your scones.
11. Place on a cookie sheet two inches apart.
12. Bake for 10 to 12 minutes or until lightly browned.

Leila's Tasteful Tips

- Make other flavors by changing the chocolate chips.
- Make other flavors by adding nuts.
- Make other flavors by changing the extract used.
- The butter, sour cream, and eggs need to remain as cold as possible to make a good dough.
- For special holiday scones, change the biscuit cutter to a three-inch shaped cookie cutter.

NO TEAPOT LEFT BEHIND

We go on our major teapot buying trips twice a year. We say it's time to, "Shop 'til you drop!" By the end of the day we certainly do drop since we can't move a muscle. Erika starts the day by saying, "Ready, set, buy, buy, buy!" Each of the companies we buy from offer drinks and food since we do not want to waste any time while looking for teapots to buy. We hold a sandwich in one hand and a teapot in the other. We get very creative and sometimes have a sandwich and soda in one hand and what we are looking to buy in the other! There is only one week to shop, so we have no time to waste. Leila is always looking for new companies and new items that would soon be added to our collection.

One day, a young man walked into our store and, thinking he was very funny, asked, "Do you have any teapots?" Erika looked around at the two-hundred plus teapots lining the walls and windows and then responded, "I'm sorry, we just ran out of teapots." The funny thing is that this question comes up at least once a week. So, Erika's quick wit is challenged often. Some customers come in just to stare at each one, as if we are a teapot museum. They have never seen so many diverse teapots under one roof. See, we told you that there are no teapots left behind!

When we first opened the tea room, Erika wanted to color coordinate the teapots and tea sets. This did not last long as we moved in hundreds of teapots. We do try to keep genres together, so all the animal teapots, tea for ones, full tea sets, and so on are together. We quickly figured out that it doesn't matter how we configure the shelves as long as we have plenty of choices. We have many manufacturers making teapots for us. When customers ask us which new teapots we are planning to order, we always reply, "All of them!". After all, what is a tea room without teapots?

When we go shopping for teapots, Erika can be on one side of the warehouse and Leila on the other, and when we meet in the middle, we are holding the same teapot. It might be in two colors, but most of the time it is the exact same item. We are two peas in a pod!

You should see our house and four storage units filled to the brim with teapots. Our inventory of teapots, tea sets, and tea accessories takes up our full house. We couldn't buy a dining room to accommodate the boxes of teapots piled high! Our garage is full, too! Erika wanted a special Shannon Irish tea set that had not been made in years. In order for the company to make it for us, we needed to buy 500 teapots, 500 teacups and saucers, 500 creamers, and 500 sugars. When we open the garage, neighbors ask if we are having a garage sale. They literally stop and stare into our garage when the door is open. We always try to close the door fast, not wanting to cause traffic hold-ups or accidents.

Today we have to order more teapots than ever before. We are never sure that we will receive all of the items that we order. If the manufacturers do not get enough buyers for that one teapot, they might decide not to make it. Erika recently called one of our manufacturers to check on one of our orders. The teapots were scheduled to be sent to us by the end of the week. The customer service manager explained that it was not economically feasible to make the shipment at this time. Erika responded, "So does that mean you don't have it in yet?" Their answer was, "Uh, huh!" It didn't seem feasible to ask when they expected the shipment. The conclusion to this story is that the order just arrived. We got the new teapots - yay! But they came several months late. Do they think that people actually buy pumpkin and ghost teapots for Christmas?

When shopping for teapots, we consider tea sets for each holiday and the tea sets for everyday use. Of course, we need and have special ones just for Christmas. We have customers who love poinsettias, reindeer, snowmen, nutcrackers, angels, and others who only want Santa. We probably have over fifty different Christmas varieties of teapots and tea sets. Christmas is by far our favorite shopping mission. Our mission, if we choose to accept it, is to leave no Christmas teapot alone on the shelf, similar to Percy, the Puny Poinsettia. We don't want any teapot to have hurt feelings. We get so excited seeing what our distributors have for us each year.

Erika grew up with the Nordstrom's mentality of selling. She can sell ice to an Eskimo. As a personal shopper, Erika spends hours in the day helping customers find their perfect teapot, tea set, or a bundle with scones and a tea set. She also spends time into the wee hours helping customers, many of whom are older women. Erika loves to talk to them and explain in detail the features of each teapot or tea set. She helps them personalize gifts and sometimes just keeps them company on the phone. Each day, Erika spends hours on the computer putting together new gift bundles from the newest teapot, tea set, cookie jar, canister, and other tea related items, then adds six scones, and a new tea sample. Erika makes each customer feel like their order is the most important one.

While writing this book, we came home from another eventful shopping spree. Leila thinks we have conquered the world of teapots. Erika would add that we conquered the world of cookie jars, too! Forget the usual Disney ones (although we did get a few), we also added new Christmas cookie jars with an upside-down reindeer, a pastel-colored snowman, a 3D poinsettia, and the biggest ornament cookie jar we have ever seen (twenty-eight inches high). We were also so excited to find some new companies to add to our playbill of tea wares. One had the most unique nutcrackers, especially Alice in Wonderland, the Wizard of Oz, and additionally Mickey and Minnie. We were so excited with all we saw and, of course, all we bought. Some of the shipments started to arrive before we arrived home. But that's ok, we are always happy to be stocked up for the next holiday and for Erika to have new bundle ideas.

Most people take vacations and actually relax. We do not know from that kind of vacation. Our vacations consist of shopping for new merchandise. The shipments are coming in daily. We need to try to keep the store clean, but some days it is just not possible. They are coming in fast and furious. One shipment can be two boxes, the next four boxes. Then comes a huge pallet of twenty plus boxes. The poor delivery man! It's a cool one hundred degrees out, so Leila gives the delivery drivers a bottle of water because they come in sweating from carrying in all of our shipments!

We can't leave Shelly's family out of our story. Shelly is an only child. That's good because we wouldn't want more than one of him roaming the earth. When Leila married Shelly in 1978, he promised her that he would never take on the traits of his father. He lied! Leila can tell you that as Shelly ages he becomes more and more like him. Shelly's father Phil was what they called a peddler. He set up a table on a street corner by a hospital in Brooklyn and peddled pocketbooks. The funny thing about Phil is that as he stood on the corner, he shouted at the passers-by, "Get your pocketbooks here, only $5.00 a pocketbook! The handles are worth 5 bucks, the zips are worth 5 bucks. Get your pocketbook today. Going fast!"

When Leila listens to Erika selling and upselling her scone bundles and tea sets, it reminds her of Phil. Leila closes her eyes, shakes her head, counts to ten, and waits for the déjà vu to come to an end. She says out loud, "Please don't let Erika take after her grandfather!" Erika says, "Look at this tea infuser mug. It costs $25.00. The lid is worth $25, the infuser is worth $25, the handle is worth $25!" Is this another of Leila's nightmares? No, it's just Erika's wonderful way of selling.

Erika and Leila went to one of the showrooms to order teapots and other tea related items. We have been buying from this company for almost ten years. In fact, this company was instrumental in having the five-hundred Shannon tea sets made for us. We recently found out that the company had been sold. We had ordered tea sets six months before and had not received anything from that order. The lady in charge of the showroom explained that it is not likely that we will get the previous order. So, looking around the showroom, we asked the woman if anything they were showing was available to be shipped. She took out a stack of papers that contained all the inventory.

Leila picked up a pretty lemon teapot. "What about this teapot and the matching items? The tea box, the sugar and creamer, the mugs, the Lazy Susans; are any of these available?" Erika asked. After looking at her log, the lady responded that she owned these products and could sell them to us. We placed a sizeable order. Erika looked at Leila puzzledly. She asked Leila quietly, "Who owns the rest of all this stuff?" Leila answered, "It's a moot point, they are not selling them to us!"

We called the customer service number provided to us to find out about our order. Erika explained that we were told that they owned the products we ordered and that everything was in stock. She went on by saying, "You told me that you own the tea paraphernalia, now I would like to own them." The customer no-service agent's response was, "We'll let you know when this might happen!" We hope someday to receive this order of tea items, but for now, it is the on-going saga of the missing teapots.

After ordering the cutest covered mugs three times, they finally arrived. There was a fox, a racoon, and an owl. Leila was cooing over her three new buddies. If

Leila had her way, each new item would have a special place in her home. Erika says they all do, one way or the other. The millions of boxes piled to the living room ceiling are evidence of this. Erika immediately started to contemplate how to set up scone and gift bundles with each of the three woodland animals. Leila frowned. "You can't separate the three, they are a Forest Family!" Leila cried.

When shopping for teapots, Erika and Leila consider a teapot for every season, for every customer, for every follower, and for every taste. Even if you are unsure of which teapot is your favorite, Erika will talk to you, get to know you, and assist you in finding the perfect teapot just for you. Being the teapot concierge she is, Erika always keeps our loyal customers coming back for their next scone and gift bundle. Our customers from all over the country reach out to us by walking-in, emails, phone calls, and even letters in response to Erika's scone and gift promotions. They order a birthday scone and teacup bundle, then a tea set and scone gift bundle, and then a holiday cookie jar and scone bundle. No matter what the occasion, Erika shows our customers that we have the perfect gift and scone bundle just for them!

To go along with your new teapot purchase, a rich and creamy treat of a gingersnap mini cheesecake is just perfection. By the way, we did buy a beautiful gingerbread house teapot that would be a perfect match!

Gingersnap Mini Cheesecakes Recipe

INGREDIENTS

2 8-ounce whipped cream cheese tubs

⅔ cups of granulated sugar

2 large eggs

2 teaspoons of pure vanilla extract

½ teaspoon of pure almond extract

1 teaspoon of ground cinnamon

1 teaspoon of ground ginger

12 gingersnap cookies (kept whole)

4 gingersnap cookies (crumbled)

2 tablespoons of butter (melted)

DIRECTIONS

1. Preheat the oven to 325 degrees F.
2. Crumble 4 of the gingersnap cookies by placing them in a ziplock bag and rolling over the cookies with a rolling pin to crumble.
3. Melt the butter in the microwave.
4. Beat the cream cheese and the sugar in a large bowl with an electric hand mixer until light and fluffy.
5. Beat in the eggs, spices, and extracts (set aside).
6. Mix the melted butter into the cookie crumbles (this will be the topping).
7. Line a 12 cup muffin tin with cupcake liners.
8. Place one of the whole cookies in each cup.
9. Fill each cup with the cream cheese mixture until it is ⅔ full.
10. Sprinkle the topping evenly on top of the 12 mini cheesecakes.
11. Bake for 22 to 24 minutes or until the edges are lightly browned.
12. When completely cooled, refrigerate overnight before serving.

Leila's Tasteful Tips

- You can use a food processor to crumble the cookies, but by using a rolling pin, you can get rid of your frustrations by taking them out on the cookies.
- Change the flavor of the cheesecake by changing the cookie bottom. Use an oreo or vanilla wafer.
- You can use a fruit topping such as blueberry, lemon, cherry, or apple. (If you do - leave out the spices, but still include the extracts).

THEMED EVENTS

There are certain days in your life that you will remember forever, such as a special birthday, your baby's birth, your wedding day (or several wedding days –we don't judge), or an anniversary . . . We are lucky enough to get to share these and other celebrations and special moments with our tea room guests. We help to create memories that last a lifetime. All these moments become part of what we do and, in turn, people remember us as part of their family. We love to enhance our guests' lives, even remotely. It is so uplifting to play just a small role in making people happy. As Dolly Parton says, "If you see someone without a smile, give them yours!"

When Leila and Shelly first got married in 1978, they had a business in New York City. This was way before Erika was born – she wasn't even a blip on the map. It was down the street from Times Square. On Friday afternoons, Shelly would stand in the line to get half-price theater tickets. They had tickets leftover from shows that did not sell out. We didn't care what show we got to see. We saw all the best Broadway shows such as Fiddler on the Roof, Shenandoah, How to Succeed, Auntie Mame, Hello Dolly, and many others, packed with the most famous actors such as Zero Mostel, Howard Keel, Carol Channing, Lucy Arnez, and Robert Morse to name a few, and the most prominent center orchestra seats. It was the best part of owning a business in New York City. We sold the business before Erika was born. We lived in the beautiful garden state of New Jersey.

For over fifteen years we had season tickets to the theatrical musicals held in New Hope, Pennsylvania. It seemed natural that Leila's love for singing and musical theater would rub off on her offspring. Erika's education with the best Broadway-type musicals, alongside her love for DVD musicals, was part of the family dynamic. Erika and Leila memorized every lyric and many famous lines. To keep Shelly awake on long car trips, we all sang our showtunes and played games guessing what famous musical a song came from. Even Charlie sang along –off key and all!

It's not unusual for Erika and Leila to suddenly burst into song, singing songs from one of their beloved television shows, old musicals, new musical movies or animated films. One small word, a character mentioned, or a well-known line is enough to stir up a whole concert in the tea room. After a long workday, it is not unusual to hear Erika and Leila harmonize some showtunes during their hour car trip home. Leila says that they are funny people. Erika replies, "Yes, you are, Mom. Funny looking!" Leila answers, "I don't understand how you can call me funny looking when you look just like me. In fact, you are my "Mini Me!"

We started our themed events as tea tastings. We paired our custom blended teas with complementing food plates. It was when we changed the tea tastings to actual themes that we saw much more interest. Yes, we did serve tea and food, but then added activities such as craft projects, solving a murder mystery, sing-alongs, trivia, and contests. All of these nuances made these events even more spectacular, and they are definitely a crowd pleaser. Most of these events sell out and sometimes we need to add a second date. People ask how to dress for these events, and we reply that the only stipulation is that clothing is not optional!

Erika starts every event with a gong roll. She has a mini gong and often cannot put it down once she starts gonging. The gong is our way of calling an event to order. We tried starting to talk to the audience and realized early on that it was hard to talk over all the chatter. The gong became a cute way to get started. Erika became addicted to the gong, or should we say gong-happy. Erika starts singing "You can ring my bell" while Leila asks her to put the gong down. It becomes necessary to send Erika away from the audience to let her gain some self control. Eventually Erika puts the gong away and the event starts.

In all the events that we put on in the tea room, Leila and Erika keep the audience in stitches by bantering back and forth. Funny things happen in the tea room. We want to start by disclosing that all we are about to tell you is completely true. We have left out the names to protect the innocent, or should we say, the not so innocent. We attract the funny, even though we are not necessarily looking for it. Erika was born a blue-eyed blonde. She is no longer blonde, but Leila tells her that she still acts blonde. Erika retorts, "Even with my blondeness I am sharper than most tools in the tool shed." What happens in the tea room, stays in the tea room!

It was our very first tea tasting event and it had been hectic all day with tables. Our event started at 6 PM after the tea room had closed, not leaving too much time to get ready. Bustling to get ready, Leila planned ten small plates as the new tea hostess prepared selected teas. Being fluffy ourselves, the new tea hostess was the poster girl for a bull in a China shop. It seemed that when we were the busiest, the strangest things happened. Erika checked on the tea hostess to see how she was doing setting up the teas and noticed there was more tea on the floor than in the pots. It's raining tea, Hallelujah!

Guests were beginning to arrive as Leila was plating her first tea pairing (usually a scone). The tea hostess entered the kitchen with a spoutless teapot with a trail of tea not far behind. The tea pot was full of tea and was now spilling out all over the white tiled floors. Leila quickly took the teapot out of the tea hostess' hands and put it into the end sink. As Shelly, the head custodian, ran for the mop, the tea hostess burst into tears. Leila stated, "I don't know why you are crying; I should be. You broke my brand-new teapot that was made in Germany. Very hard to replace, since it is an antique!"

Leila quickly found out that the tea hostess did not have a sense of humor. She started to cry so loudly and then ran into the lady's room and locked herself in. Erika tried to get the tea hostess out of the bathroom as she cajoled her to come out. It finally happened, and our guests applauded our handling of the situation. Now we can definitely look back on this and laugh. Today, it's a comedy of errors, but back then it was more of a tragedy. Bump, bump, bump; a teapot bites the dust!

Let us now describe our themed events to let you in on exactly what we do. These events define Erika's Tea Room as a celebration place for all those who attend!

BABY AND BRIDAL SHOWERS, BIRTHDAYS, REHEARSAL DINNERS, AND SMALL WEDDINGS

Erika starts each of these events by sitting down with the party planners and planning everything, starting with a personalized menu, favors, and décor. Erika assists in all decisions, providing many options to choose from. When Erika has completed the meeting, Leila takes over with planning the recipes.

We always imagined our tea room as a special celebration place for birthdays and other special occasions. We have the same people coming to the tea room annually to celebrate their birthday or their anniversary. Right after we opened, we met an eccentric formidable hat lady named Ruby. She was a no-holds-barred, say-it-like-it-is woman of eighty. Ruby and Leila hit it off right away. Ruby was opinionated and didn't hesitate to give advice, even if it was not solicited. Ruby would tell Leila to change the tea room to a cafe or to hang a huge teapot sign from the roof. Leila always acknowledged Ruby's suggestions but told her that she was not going to follow them. That is why they got along so swimmingly. Now to move on to Ruby's celebration. Ruby wanted to plan three birthday parties for herself. One was for her nearest and dearest friends, around ten ladies. The second was for other friends and some relatives, around twenty guests. Lastly, the third party was for Ruby to invite people she sat on various boards with, hob-knobbed with, and lorded over, around thirty guests.

Ruby was very particular with each menu. She wanted seating charts and place cards. Ruby wanted us to do her invitations and specified that all should be wearing appropriate formal dress garb including hats. Each celebration was different yet so much fun to plan. We are not sure who had a better time: Ruby or us!

We've hosted many bridal showers over the years since opening. There are a few that stand out from the rest. The first one Leila and Erika remember was a lingerie bridal shower. From the onset we saw that the mother-in-law was not friendly to the bride. There was a lot of snickering and whispering coming from her throughout the shower. All the guests brought slinky, silky items for the new bride-to-be. Then the bride opened the mother-in-law's gift. The gift was a one-piece flannel adult onesie with attached feet. Anyone could see that this mother-in-law, or should we say monster-in-law, was going to be instrumental in contributing to a long and happy marriage!

We had another, very different, mother-in-law and daughter-in-law enjoying each other's company while they relished in their afternoon tea experience. They decided on two teas they both liked so that they could try two different ones and also shared their chosen desserts. The mother-in-law told us about her special, beautiful daughter-in-law. It was so nice watching their loving bond. This is how this relationship should be.

Another bridal shower we hosted was for a typical bridezilla. She definitely defined what a bridezilla actually is. While Erika was helping her plan the menu, the bridezilla could not make a decision. She came back six times to make changes to the menu, each time asking additional questions and making other demands. She wanted fresh flowers instead of our silk ones we make to match the tablecloths. She wanted to move her bedroom furniture into the tea room, so that her friends could play dress up.

The day of the shower, the bridezilla arrived 2 ½ hours late. Her bridal party started drinking before they arrived and were rather drunk. We normally allow two to three hours for a bridal shower and had an additional bridal shower planned for later that day. They started to arrive when the bridezilla finally entered. The second bridal shower's group was so lovely that they did not mind. In the end, everything worked out and both showers were a success.

It is very hard to get a venue for a very small wedding. Typically, the minimum number of people is fifty. We had known the bride, Connie, and her daughter, Shanna, for a few years prior. Connie was filling us in on her plans and told us about her inability to book a place to host the wedding and reception. Leila told her that we could handle the wedding and could create a menu to host the reception dinner. Of course, we started with a homemade scone with Devon cream. We were determined to make Connie's wedding day memorable. We helped the bride get ready in the back of the store before the guests started to arrive.

Instead of the typical tea room food, Erika planned a custom menu and Leila made the couple a special cake of their choosing. From the back of the tea room to the dining room, there was a nice long aisle for Connie to walk down. Connie's beautiful white bridal gown was a vision in white. It was so lovely!

There was a minister that conducted a short but sweet ceremony and then all sat down at the tables. A champagne toast was followed by dinner served in courses. To this day, when we see Connie, we reminisce about her special wedding day and our part in making it a memorable occasion.

The menu started with Kahlua and Cream scones. Then we served an italian wedding soup with tiny turkey meatballs. The main course was a baked chicken cutlet with a lemon butter sauce served over wide buttered noodles. For dessert, Leila made a french vanilla cake with a cannoli cream topping. We made all of Connie's favorites and her dreams come true.

Baked Chicken Cutlets with a Lemon Butter Sauce Recipe

INGREDIENTS

One thinly sliced boneless chicken cutlet per person (if the cutlets are small, make two)

½ cup regular mayonnaise

½ cup italian-style breadcrumbs with cheese

1 teaspoon ground pepper

1 teaspoon garlic powder

1 teaspoon onion powder

SAUCE

¼ cup unsalted butter (melted)

¼ teaspoon sea salt

1 teaspoon minced garlic

2 Tablespoons fresh lemon juice

1 Tablespoon grated lemon peel

½ teaspoon ground black pepper

½ teaspoon onion powder

DIRECTIONS

1. Preheat the oven to 375 degrees F.
2. Cover a cookie sheet with parchment paper.
3. Whisk together the mayonnaise and spices. Set aside.
4. Put the breadcrumbs on a flat plate.
5. Melt the butter in the microwave.
6. Whisk the butter, the lemon juice, the lemon peel, and the spices together. Set aside.
7. Brush each cutlet with mayonnaise and then roll in the breadcrumbs.
8. Bake for 15 minutes, then turn over and bake for an additional 10 minutes.
9. Pour the sauce over the top and put in the oven for another 10 minutes or until fully browned and crisp.

Leila's Tasteful Tips

- We served the chicken cutlets over a bed of buttered noodles. This would be great over rice or mashed potatoes as well.
- You can substitute veal cutlets instead of the chicken.
- You can substitute tomato sauce instead of lemon butter sauce.

VARIETIES OF ACTUAL THEMED EVENTS – MURDER MYSTERY, GONE WITH THE WIND, DRAG SHOW, GREASE, ELVIS SING-A-LONG, PLUS MANY MORE

Erika thinks about interesting themes for our murder mystery events. Leila takes whatever theme she comes up with and then writes the script for the murder mystery. Like everything we do, Leila and Erika never disappoint. Every event is spectacular! When writing a murder mystery, Leila needs to consider the number of characters in the story, who was murdered, how the victim was murdered, and the reason for the murder. When Erika chooses the theme, she also develops the menu, but not without Leila stating that she had not approved the menu, even though she always does! Leila just likes to give Erika a hard time.

The very first murder mystery was "Murder at Erika's Tea Room." We decided to start the series of murder mysteries right in the tea room. As the story goes, Erika found out that day that Leila was not her real mother. The victim was her mother. For weeks after the event, Erika was asked if Leila was her real mother. This event confused many of our usual customers. It was so fun to figure out whether the victim was murdered by poison, a fatal blow, gunshot, or by some other tragic means. Even though Leila wrote the story one way, the guests could take it in many different directions, so Leila had to think fast on her feet to either get everyone back on track or go with the flow and let the audience come to their own conclusions. At the end of the evening, the group voted on whodunnit!

The menu consisted of:

Death by Chocolate Scone
Bloody Good Red Bean and Rice Soup
Fowl Play Chicken
Caramel Crypt Apple Cake

Fowl Play Chicken Recipe

INGREDIENTS

1-pound fresh chicken cutlets (2 large) cooked and cubed

1 32-ounce low sodium chicken stock

1 cup Ritz crackers, crushed

½ cup of flour

1 teaspoon of each garlic powder, onion powder and pepper (or two if you like it spicier)

1 12-ounce steamable bag of frozen mixed vegetables

3 large eggs

1 cup heavy cream

1 8-ounce package of triple cheddar shredded cheese

DIRECTIONS

1. Preheat the oven to 350 degrees F.
2. Cook the chicken in stock until fork-tender.
3. Cool the chicken and cube – set aside.
4. Steam the frozen veggies in the microwave for six minutes – set aside to cool.
5. In a large bowl, whisk the eggs, heavy cream, and spices.
6. Add flour and whisk until all the lumps are out.
7. Add the cooked chicken to the mixture.
8. Fold in half of the cheese.
9. Put the mixture in a 8x11 inch casserole dish.
10. Top with crushed Ritz crackers, then sprinkle with the remaining cheese.
11. Bake for 30 minutes or until nice and brown.

Leila's Tasteful Tips

- You can substitute the cheddar cheese for another shredded cheese (mozzarella, gouda, or swiss).
- Instead of heavy cream, use Half-and-Half or milk.
- You can substitute any other steamable vegetable (broccoli, carrots, peas, etc).
- You can use an 8x11 disposable pan.

Another very exciting murder mystery we wrote centered on the hit TV show, *Gilligan's Island*. We called it "Return to Gilligan's Island." Let's preempt the start of this murder mystery by asking all of you some questions: 1) If the professor was able to build a robot then why couldn't he find a way to get off the island? 2) If the Skipper was able to build all the huts and the furniture then why couldn't he repair the ship? And lastly: 3) How did all the visitors get on and off Gilligan's Island? Why couldn't they get the rest of them home? So now that we have (mostly) established the setting, we need to find out who was killed, why the murder took place, and how it happened.

Erika called all to order with her famous gong, while Leila handed out the roles. Leila typed the character list, the setting, and some questions that needed to be answered. She explained how we were going to solve the murder mystery in between each course that was going to be served. Erika explained how we would look for clues and elected one of the attendees as the inspector to keep everyone on track. Leila handed out secret notes to steer the characters in the right direction. Around the time of dessert, a show of hands voted on which suspect did it, with what, and for what reason.

The menu consisted of:

The Professor's Pina Colada Scone
Mr. Howell's Fruit and Nut Salad
Ginger's Honey Chicken and Rice
Gilligan's Banana Cream Pie

Banoffee Pie Recipe
(Gilligan's Banana Cream Pie)

INGREDIENTS

15-ounce box of Vanilla Wafers

2 boxes of banana instant pudding

2 ½ cups cold milk

2 cups cold heavy cream

4 yellow bananas peeled and thinly sliced

Caramel ice cream topping

DIRECTIONS

1. In a bowl, using an electric mixer, make 1 box of the pudding with milk (pudding).

2. In another bowl, using an electric mixer, make the other pudding with the heavy cream (topping).

3. Peel and slice the banana.

4. Smash all the vanilla cookies in a zip lock bag.

5. Assemble individual portions by layering the ingredients and refrigerate for at least an hour.

6. Layer the pudding from the bottom with cookie crumbs, caramel, pudding, bananas, and then repeat –cookie crumbs, caramel, bananas, topping.

Leila's Tasteful Tips

- Do not slice the bananas too far in advance or they will brown.
- You can make this in as many layers as you want.
- Change the whole taste by using strawberry instant puddings and fresh strawberries.

Crystal Chandelier came to the tea room to put on a drag-show themed event. When we first met with Philip, he asked how risqué he could be. We explained that a tea room doesn't lend itself to risqué and on a scale from 1 to 10, we said that he should stay in the range of 3 or less. If he was a 3, we couldn't imagine what the higher numbers might bring. Crystal brought in a rack of costume changes. He did extraordinary impersonations of Rocky from The Rocky Horror Picture Show and Cher. He lip-synched to the best. One performance stood out from the rest. Dressed as Tina Turner, he came out from the back, pushing a walker. Turning to face the audience, the walker became a portable potty. He pulled out a roll of toilet tissue, papered the seat, sat down and sang: "I need a private bathroom, bathroom for money, when you have to go number two . . ." It was the funniest thing you ever saw or heard!

In the audience was an 80+ year-old man. We were watching Crystal play Rocky as the music played, "I'm just a Sweet Transvestite". To play it up, she/he put her size 15 thigh-high red patent leather boot on the man's knee. Leila was terrified that the man would have a stroke. The man was elated. A great time was had by all. It was one of our most popular events.

The menu consisted of:

Fruit and Nut Scone
Sausage, Peppers, and Onion Quiche
Vegetarian Lasagna
Thin Mint Trifle

Vegetarian Lasagna Recipe

INGREDIENTS

1 16-ounce box of rigatoni pasta

1 medium green squash unpeeled, washed, and thoroughly dried

1 15-ounce steamable sliced carrots

1 32-ounce traditional pasta Sauce

1 32-ounce ricotta cheese

2 8-ounce shredded mozzarella cheese

DIRECTIONS

1. Preheat the oven to 375 degrees F.
2. Cook the pasta as directed on the box until al dente. Strain and set aside.
3. Mix 1/3 of the pasta sauce into the pasta.
4. Cut the ends off the squash and slice thinly on a mandolin.
5. Steam carrots and place on a paper towel to cool.
6. In a 9x11 inch lasagna pan or a disposable pan, pour 1/3 of the pasta sauce.
7. Place a thin layer of the pasta on the bottom.
8. Evenly spread the squash and carrots.
9. Evenly put teaspoons of ricotta cheese and sprinkle with mozzarella.
10. Dot with the pasta sauce.
11. Start the next layer with pasta and repeat steps 7,8, and 9.
12. End with a layer of pasta and then spread the remaining sauce on the top.
13. Cover with foil and bake for 1 hour.

Leila's Tasteful Tips

- You can use any of your favorite vegetables.
- You can also make this without any vegetables.
- Instead of using rigatoni, you can use lasagna.
- For gluten-free – use gluten-free pasta.

Our "Gone with the Wind the Continuation" event started with a story Leila wrote. As we left off, Scarlett asks Rhett Butler to stay and when he tells her he will not, she replies, "Where should I go, what should I do?" To which Rhett replies, "Frankly my dear, I don't give a damn." Leila and Erika divide the audience into two. Leila leads one half and Erika the other. Leila says to her group, "Everytime we say *Scarlett*, you will say, 'After all, tomorrow is another day'." Erika says to her group, "Every time we say *Rhett*, you will say, 'Frankly my dear, I don't give a damn'."

Rhett has left Scarlett at the door. 'I know what to do', she says. 'I will make new clothes with the brand-new curtains in the kitchen. Rhett will see me with those cute cherries and my spring bonnet and then fall back in love with me all over again.' We hear Mammy shuffling over with her red pantaloons making lots of weird noises as she enters. Scarlett asks Mammy to get Rhett back so she can talk him into staying. He arrives shortly after.

Rhett asks, "Scarlett, what's wrong? The only thing you ever cared about is you, just you, only you and, of course, Tara." Scarlett responds, "No, Rhett, that's not true. I love you; I need you; I can't live without you and, of course, your money. And someone who can dress me, cook for me, and take care of me!" Rhett turns to leave, intending to never return. Scarlett yells after him, "Where should I go, what should I do?" Rhett retorts, "Finally, Scarlett, leave me alone since I truly don't give a damn!" Erika and Leila sing in unison, "Da, Da, Da, Da – Da, Da, Da, Da". The end.

After we warmed up the audience with the story, Leila served the main course, and then afterwards, Erika asked trivia questions. This was such a fun event that we pull it out of mothballs time and time again.

The menu consisted of:

Melanie's Sweet as Pie Sweet Potato Scone
Prissy's I Don't Know How to Birth no Baby Watermelon Soup
Scarlett's I'll Never Go Hungry Again Barbeque Plate
Rhett's I don't Give a Damn Bourbon Pecan Tea Bread

Rhett's I Don't Give a Damn Bourbon Pecan Tea Bread Recipe

CAKE INGREDIENTS

½ cup strong brewed Bourbon tea

2 Tablespoons dark molasses

¾ cup brown sugar

¾ teaspoon cinnamon

1 ½ cup all-purpose flour

½ teaspoon baking powder

½ teaspoon baking soda

½ teaspoon salt

½ cup chopped pecans

¼ cup raisins

½ cup unsalted butter (melted)

1 large egg

GLAZE INGREDIENTS

1 cup confectioners' sugar

½ teaspoon pure vanilla extract

½ teaspoon melted butter

2 Tablespoons Bourbon tea

DIRECTIONS

1. Preheat the oven to 350 degrees F. Using baking spray, spray the bottom and up the sides of a 9x13 inch baking pan or disposable pan.

2. Combine raisins, molasses, and hot tea in a small bowl. Set aside for at least 10 minutes.

3. Mix together the dry ingredients.

4. In a large bowl, mix the butter, sugar, and egg with a hand mixer until fluffy.

5. Add the dry ingredients to the wet above.

6. Mix in the raisin mixture.

7. Fold in the pecans.

8. Spread the batter evenly in the baking pan. Bake for 30 minutes or until a cake tester comes out clean.

9. While the cake is baking, make the glaze.

10. As soon as the cake comes out of the oven, spread the glaze over the top. Let it cool before serving.

Leila's Tasteful Tips

- Change the tea flavor to change the cake flavor.
- Change the raisins to another dried fruit.
- Change the nuts to chocolate chips.
- Change molasses to 2 Tablespoons spiced rum or a flavored bourbon.

We couldn't leave Shelly out of these themed events. Shelly mostly has to clean up after everything is done and everyone has left. He is an integral part of many of the events. In the Queen's Garden Party, Shelly played the Queen. Everyone wanted a picture with the Queen. Leila felt he looked too much like his mother and hated him all day, until his wig and makeup was washed away. In the Wizard of Oz, Shelly played the Cowardly Lion and led the audience in the sing-a-long "If I was King of the Forest." In the Japanese Tea Ceremony, Shelly played one ugly Geisha. But the most memorable character Shelly has played was Tiny Waikiki, the best (or worst) hula dancer you have ever seen.

We were expecting a dance teacher to come teach hula lessons to the audience. She ran a dance studio down the street, but she had to bow out at the last minute. Thus, Tiny Waikiki was born. As Leila read the moves of the hula from the internet, Shelly/Tiny demonstrated. His grass skirt kept falling off and his cockeyed coconuts were hysterical. Leila and Erika realized that Shelly finally achieved his full potential with his portrayal of Tiny Waikiki, the hula dancer extraordinaire.

The menu consisted of:

Toasted Coconut and Papaya Scone
Barbeque Stuffed Sweet Potato
Kona Dog
Pina Colada Cheesecake

Barbeque Stuffed Sweet Potato Recipe

INGREDIENTS

4 large sweet potatoes (washed and ends removed)

1 1-pound pork loin

1 32-ounce low sodium chicken stock

1 cup honey barbeque sauce

2 Tablespoons cinnamon

¼ cup unsalted butter (1/2 stick) melted

¼ cup chopped pecans

DIRECTIONS

1. Preheat the oven to 375 degrees F.

2. Line a cookie sheet with parchment paper.

3. Wash the sweet potatoes and wrap them in paper towels.

4. Microwave for 10 minutes or until soft.

5. Cut each sweet potato lengthwise.

6. Scoop out the middle of each sweet potato.

7. In a bowl, mix the pork loin, melted butter, barbeque sauce, and sweet potato center.

8. Refill the sweet potato halves with the mixture and assemble on a cookie sheet.

9. Sprinkle with the pecans and cinnamon.

10. Bake for 30 minutes or until a light crust forms.

Leila's Tasteful Tips

- You can substitute chicken for pork loin.
- You can use large baking potatoes instead of sweet potatoes.
- You can add a dollop of sour cream to each potato after it is baked.

VARIETIES OF HOLIDAY EVENTS –MOTHER'S DAY, VALENTINE'S DAY, ST. PATRICK'S DAY, HALLOWEEN, BLACK FRIDAY, EASTER

Holidays give Erika opportunities to reach deep into her creative toolbox and pull out imaginative menus. She comes up with very special ideas that complement the season or holiday. Then Leila creates her own recipes and ingredients to elevate Erika's genius. Erika grew up with holidays celebrated in her home, where the "Need to Feed" culminated. Leila loved cooking on the auspicious occasions, wanting each to be more special than the next. Let us share some of the past menus. Of course, we will also share a few of the recipes, too!

Our events fill up fast and at times we have to open up another seating or day. Returning guests make these events an annual tradition. Erika and Leila look forward to seeing our regulars and love to make completely different menus so that nothing gets stale (literally!). We would like to share some menus from the holiday's past. A trip down memory lane!

MOTHER'S DAY

Mother's Day was always the day that Leila, Erika, and Charlie could spend quality time together doing what they loved to do. We sought out new tea rooms to share our passion together. It was a time to share laughter, private jokes, and good food. With this always in mind, Leila and Erika wanted to impart these wonderful traditions with existing and new guests. Our Mother's Day menus are notorious for being extra special and we love to see the familiar faces year after year. Even though Mother's Day is months away, we can't wait to plan this year's monumental menu.

A previous menu consisted of:

Pear and Almond Scone
Chilled Avocado Soup
Mediterranean Shrimp Skewer
Sandwiches - Asian Chicken Salad, Tarragon Egg, Roasted Carrot Hummus
Honey Almond Tartlet

Roasted Carrot Hummus Recipe

INGREDIENTS

1 8-ounce bag of fresh baby carrots

1 whole garlic, peeled and separated into cloves

1 32-ounce can of garbanzo beans (chickpeas)

½ cup extra virgin olive oil

2 teaspoons of each salt, garlic powder, onion powder, and ground black pepper

DIRECTIONS

1. Preheat the oven to 400 degrees F.
2. Mix half of the olive oil (1/4 cup) with carrots and garlic gloves.
3. Bake until carrots and garlic are soft and browned (approximately 30 minutes).
4. Rinse the garbanzo beans and get rid of any skins.
5. Using a large food processor, grind the garbanzo beans.
6. Then add the cooked carrot mixture.
7. Add the remaining olive oil and continue grinding until you achieve your desired consistency.
8. Add condiments.
9. Cool before serving.

Leila's Tasteful Tips

- Add roasted red peppers for another great taste.
- Add kalamata olives for an alternate flavor.
- Serve on small breads such as French bread or large crackers.

VALENTINE'S DAY

Valentine's Day is a day of sharing love. At Erika's Tea Room we believe we share love with our food. They always say that, "The way to a man's heart is through his stomach." This is exactly how Leila landed Sheldon. Now, after forty-five years of marital bliss, Leila wants to know what she can do to reverse this spell. Leila wants to know what the return policy is after all these years? But then again, who will wash the dishes?

Every year, Valentine's Day is a day to plan a very special menu. We want to share our passion and love through the foods served. Erika plans a love-filled menu consisting of chocolate and decadent foods. Whether you are sharing the dish with your favorite someone or being stingy and enjoying it solo, you will love the delicacies served. Don't worry, we never plan the same menu twice. Amore, amore - please give me some more, hey!

A previous menu consisted of:

Lemon Meringue Scone
Sweet Potato Soup
Bacon Ranch Chicken Salad Croissant
Asparagus and Gruyère Quiche
Chocolate Banoffee Pie

Easy Bacon Ranch Chicken Salad Recipe

INGREDIENTS

2 large chicken breasts

1 32-ounce low sodium chicken stock

2 Tablespoons mayonnaise

½ cup ranch salad dressing

¼ cup Hormel 40% lean bacon bits

1 teaspoon of each – onion powder, garlic powder, and ground black pepper

DIRECTIONS

1. Boil chicken breasts in stock until fork-tender (approximately 1 hour) and leave to cool.

2. Shred the chicken.

3. Mix the dressing, bacon, mayo, and spices into the chicken.

4. Refrigerate overnight.

Leila's Tasteful Tips

- Instead of bacon, add dried cranberries.
- Serve on your favorite bread (or croissant).
- Instead of ranch dressing, try Thousand Island dressing for a new twist.

ST. PATRICK'S DAY

Corned beef and cabbage can be served in many creative ways. It is Erika's menu and Leila's recipes that can take up the challenge of putting a unique spin on all the recipes. The "Luck of the Irish" is always with you at Erika's Tea Room; from the start with a Bailey's Irish Cream Tea until the wonderful conclusion of a Bailey's Irish Cream Cheesecake. Leila loves to take the conventional Irish foods and make them her own. Even though we are not Irish, there is always room for a good lean corned beef sandwich on our family's table. In fact, we never met a corned beef we didn't like.

A previous menu consisted of:

Chocolate Guinness Scone
Cream of Cabbage Soup
Ham and Potato Quiche
Corned Beef Slider
Bailey's Irish Cream Cheesecake

Corned Beef Slider Recipe

INGREDIENTS

Flat-cut fresh corned beef

1 32-ounce low sodium chicken stock

1 small red cabbage

1 small red onion

2 Tablespoons canola oil

2 Tablespoons apple cider vinegar

½ cup mayonnaise

2 teaspoons of each – onion powder, garlic powder, and black ground pepper

Small, crusty rolls

DIRECTIONS

1. Wash the corned beef to remove all remaining corning spices.
2. In a large stock pot, put the corned beef and cover with the stock.
3. Boil until fork-tender (1 to 1 ½ hours).
4. Cool before slicing (slice to desired thickness).
5. Shred the cabbage.
6. Peel and dice the onion.
7. In a frying pan, put in the oil and then fry the cabbage and onion until soft and caramelized. Allow to cool.
8. In a bowl, mix the cabbage and onion with mayo, vinegar, and spices.
9. Cut open the crusty roll.
10. Put a slice of corned beef on the roll and then cover with cabbage slaw.

Leila's Tasteful Tips

- You can add a touch of Dijon mustard to the slaw to add some tanginess.
- You can add a slice of Swiss cheese to make a Reuben sandwich.

HALLOWEEN

Halloween brings out the eeriness of the fall season. The table linens are changed to pumpkins as Erika brings in the wonderful Pumpkin and Apple Spiced Teas. Erika makes sure the menus share all Halloween's bewitching flavors. Then Leila comes up with spooktacular recipes that are deadly good. Whether you arrive at the tea room on your favorite broom or headless horse, Erika's Tea Room is sure to please with this spirited menu.

A previous menu consisted of:

Maple Pecan Scone
Butternut Squash Soup
Apple Pecan Chicken Salad Croissant
Pumpkin Deviled Egg Salad Sandwich
Candied Carrot Quiche
Caramel Candy Monkey Bread

Caramel Candy Monkey Bread Recipe

INGREDIENTS

1 can refrigerated Grand biscuits

1 package of Rolo chocolate caramel candy – you will need 32 pieces (peel off the foil wrapper!)

½ stick unsalted butter, melted

2 Tablespoons cinnamon

½ cup granulated sugar

8 cupcake papers

DIRECTIONS

1. Preheat the oven to 350 degrees F.

2. Place the cupcake papers in muffin tins (makes 8).

3. Using a pizza cutter or a sharp knife, cut the 8 Grand biscuits into 4 pieces.

4. Take each section, open, and place a Rolo in the middle, then form a ball.

5. In a bowl, mix the cinnamon into sugar.

6. Dip the ball in butter and then roll it in the sugar.

7. Put four balls into each cup.

8. Bake for 15 to 20 minutes or until browned.

Leila's Tasteful Tips

- You can put a drizzle of chocolate or caramel syrup on top of each monkey bread before baking.
- You can add some dried fruits or nuts on each monkey bread before baking.
- Serve hot and add a scoop of vanilla ice cream.

BLACK FRIDAY

After your day of shopping, missing out on the department store's promotion items, come relax at Erika's Tea Room. Avoid the mobs, get your gifts wrapped for free, and enjoy a pleasurable meal. Erika is the best gift wrapper. She uses an enormous amount of tape, patches wrapping paper together, and might have to wrap it more than once, but once finished, the gifts will look like they were wrapped badly and with oodles of love. We do everything with homemade charm! Erika wants to ensure that it looks like you wrapped it personally. Just joking!

When Erika was a little girl, Leila slept outside Bradley's Department Store to get one of the first talking Cabbage Patch Kid dolls. When they finally opened the doors at 8 AM, Leila was pushed through the doors, her feet not touching the floor, until she landed in front of the dolls she wanted. A week later, she was so happy to give Erika her new doll for Hanukkah. Leila pressed the button to make the doll talk to Erika. Erika's eyes opened wide and then she started to cry. Erika was so scared that the doll was tossed in the closet, never to be seen or heard from again. The moral of this story is: Don't fight the crowds, come to Erika's Tea Room instead and shop small.

A previous menu consisted of:

Cranberry Pistachio Scone
Corn Chowder
Turkey and Dressing Sandwich
Potato and Bacon Quiche
Pumpkin Cannoli

Corn Chowder Recipe

INGREDIENTS

1 16-ounce can of diced potatoes (rinsed)

2 12-ounce bags of frozen sweetcorn

2 15-ounce cans of creamed corn

1 32-ounce low sodium chicken stock

1 16-ounce heavy cream

2 teaspoons of each – green parsley, onion powder, garlic powder, and black ground pepper

DIRECTIONS

1. Put all the ingredients except the heavy cream into a medium stock pot.
2. Bring to a boil, then turn down the heat.
3. Add the heavy cream.
4. Keep simmering the soup until you are ready to serve.

Leila's Tasteful Tips

- You can put in diced cooked chicken to make a chicken corn chowder.
- You can put in diced red peppers to create a Southwestern flair.
- Taste, and add additional spices if needed.

EASTER

Hop over to Erika's Tea Room for one of our tea room eggstraordinares. Erika loves to play with the classic Easter foods when preparing the menu. Leila is eggstatic about all the wonderful flavors. Our first year open was the first time Leila ever made a ham. Growing up in a semi-kosher home, Leila never had ham. So, when we looked at the main meats served, ham was a mainstay. Leila quickly called a close friend and he explained how to make a glazed ham. We have to tell you the truth, the first year, Leila overcooked the ham and it tasted like roast pork! The glaze was delicious though. Erika taste tested the ham and was amazed at how good ham was. She thought Leila had been hiding this decadent treat from her all her life. Now, Leila is an expert at making spiral hams and all the guests give their compliments to the chef.

A previous menu consisted of:

Almond Joy Scone
Carrot and Orzo Soup
Sweet Potato Quiche
Cherry Glazed Ham Sandwich
Orange Panna Cotta

Orange Panna Cotta Recipe (Gluten-free)

CRUST INGREDIENTS:

½ cup pecan meal

2 Tablespoons butter (melted)

2 teaspoons cinnamon

2 Tablespoons orange zest (fresh or glazed)

FILLING INGREDIENTS:

1 14-ounce can sweetened condensed milk

2 large eggs (yolks only)

½ cup orange juice

DIRECTIONS:

1. Preheat the oven 350 degrees F.
2. Line a cupcake pan with seven baking cups.
3. Melt the butter in the microwave (1 minute).
4. Mix the pecan meal, butter, zest, and cinnamon.
5. Put 1 teaspoon of the pecan mixture into each cup and press together.
6. Using a whisk, beat the eggs and milk.
7. Add the orange juice.
8. Evenly add the wet ingredients into the baking cups.
9. Bake for 15 minutes or until set, then refrigerate for at least 2 hours (preferably overnight).

Leila's Tasteful Tips

- To make a lime panna cotta, use ½ cup of pure lime juice.
- Keep the egg whites in the fridge to make meringue cookies.
- Instead of pecan meal for the crust, use a vanilla wafer or shortbread cookie.

GROUP EVENTS – RED HAT LADIES, MEMORY CARE FACILITIES, CHURCH GROUPS, BOOK CLUBS, QUILTING CLUBS, VIRTUAL EVENTS, COOKING CLASSES

A memory care facility coming to Erika's Tea Room – Oh, boy! Once a year, the local memory care facility buses in a group for a tea luncheon. Erika holds open the door as Leila helps seat the twenty plus walker-toting arrivals. Immediately after seating, our tea barista pours the first tea while Leila gives each attendee their scone of the day. Then each person gets their own plate of finger sandwiches and soup. Mildred always pulls the strings of Leila's heart by asking if the plate of food placed in front of her is hers alone or does she have to share it. Leila loves to tell her that the food is all hers and if she does not finish it, she can take home what's left over. Leila also assures Mildred that after she has finished her lunch, there is a delicious dessert waiting for her.

At another table, Joe spreads the linen napkin on his lap. Then he proceeds to take the small teaspoon, sugar tongs, sugar cubes, and sandwich and fold them into the napkin. Erika goes over to Joe and explains that if he takes those things out of the tea room then we will not have it for him the next time he comes. Erika tries to keep an eye on him for the remainder of the time the group is in the tea room.

Once the group has finished their meal, the activities director leads them across the street to the thrift store. Remember the scene from "The Producers" where the old ladies dance in the street with their walkers? The twenty plus attendees walk slowly across the street clutching their walkers. Leila runs to the middle of the road to stop the traffic so that no one gets hurt, then Leila returns to the tea room. Mildred comes out of the lady's room and starts to cry. "I don't believe they left me here again!" Erika assures her that she will take Mildred to where the group is. We said goodbye to Mildred, until we see her again next year.

We also host off-site cooking and baking classes. At one of the adult communities, we hosted a "Baking with Tea" event. Leila was demonstrating how to make the best Chai Doodle cookies. With one hand she cracked her egg into a small bowl. Brenda, an attendee, was so excited by this. "Please show me that again," she exclaimed. Leila did it one more time. Brenda wanted Leila to show it to her a third time, but only two eggs were required. Erika chimed in by saying, "Break an egg, not a leg, let the yolk drip down!" Leila quickly told Erika that this was not a joke for an adult community — too many people with brittle bones.

Sometimes we confuse our guests with our banter. Erika might say, "Mom, you got some 'splainin to do!" Desi said this to Lucy when she got into trouble. This might come out of nowhere, because we understand the context of what we are saying to each other. We always understand each other's references, but the guests might not. If the guests look puzzled, we then explain.. On occasion, a guest has an epiphany and gets what we say from the start. These are our kind of people!

Chai Doodle Cookies Recipe

INGREDIENTS

2 ¾ cups all purpose flour

1 cup brown sugar

1 Tablespoon loose leaf chai tea

½ teaspoon salt

1 teaspoon baking soda

2 teaspoons cream of tartar

1 Tablespoon cinnamon

1 teaspoon ginger

¼ teaspoon nutmeg

¼ teaspoon black pepper

1 cup granulated sugar

2 eggs

1 cup or 2 sticks of butter (melted)

DIRECTIONS

1. Preheat the oven to 350 degrees.
2. Melt the butter in a microwave-safe bowl for 1 minute.
3. Add the sugar to the butter and whisk until fluffy.
4. Whisk the eggs into the mixture.
5. Combine the dry ingredients into another bowl.
6. Mix the wet ingredients into the dry ingredients.
7. Line a cookie sheet with parchment paper.
8. Using a cookie scoop, place the cookies 2 inches apart.
9. Bake for 15 to 18 minutes or until lightly browned.

Leila's Tasteful Tips

1. Bake for less time for a softer cookie, or more time for a crispier cookie. Just not until burnt!
2. Substitute the chai tea for a pumpkin spice tea for a fall flavor.
3. These make a great base for vanilla ice cream. Add some chocolate or caramel sauce on top of the ice cream.

PIVOTING OUR BUSINESS

If Darwin was around today, his theory of "Survival of the Fittest" would be so relevant. As far as we can see, we only have two choices: survive or go under. As we like to say, we had to put all our scones in one basket and move full throttle into shipping them nationwide. Erika and Leila sing their song proudly, "We will survive, we will survive, as long as we have our scones, we know we can survive!"

The world has changed in the last few years while writing our book. In business you need to "Pivot or Get off the Pot". We never understood the meaning of the word, "pivot" until recently. Ballet dancers pivot on their toes, and businesses must do the same. You need to stay on your toes, and pivot as needed. It seems that mostly everyone is doing their shopping online these days. They do not want to get out of their pajamas. It seems that walking into a physical store is becoming passé.

Economic times have taken their toll on the tea room business. When we started, we were open six days a week, served from 11 AM until 4 PM and had full days of tables. We knew that we had to add a new dimension to our business to survive changing times. Having some downtime gave us the opportunity to assess what our strengths are and where we would like to be in the future. If life gives you lemons, make lemonade and lemon scones and lemon cupcakes! You get the picture. We strongly believe that if something gets in our way, we can figure out another way, together!

We quickly pivoted the business from mostly tables and walk-in retail to shipping. We needed to go to reservations required so that we could accommodate all of our special customers. The other day a customer told us, "I don't like the idea of making reservations! Last minute I might not be able to come. . ." Thus the need to change.

We ship scone subscriptions, birthday scone bundles, tea set and scone bundles, gift baskets with scones, corporate gifts with scones, and holiday scone bundles, to name just a few of our pivoting ideas. Let's start by saying, 'If you keep doing what you have always done, you will continue to get the same results.' Let's change our work model to get better outcomes. Don't put yourself into just one box. Either expand the box to include more, or put yourself into multiple boxes. More choices, more opportunities await. A cliché that fits this very experience: "Don't box yourself in, have wings to fly!" There are no limits to what you can do.

Leila is very proud of Erika's creativity. Leila is in awe of how easily it seems to be for Erika to generate one promotion after the other on a daily basis. We know how important it is to stay at the top of our dear friends' minds. Erika creates innovative events to fill tables in the tea room. The latest event, "Bee a little Craft Tea at Erika's Tea Room" is one of Erika's craft events. Every attendee will get a "I like big cups and I just can't lie" tea towel to bejewel and a three-course luncheon as well. Erika and Leila entertain the guests with their fun-filled banter during these events. Then Erika continues her communication with a new tea set bundle. She adds, "Bee ready for any occasion with this Bee Blossom tea set!" Again, isn't this an exceptional way to display our newest purchase and scone flavor?

When Leila was little her family spent summers in the bungalow colonies in the Catskill Mountains in New York. Leila's mom Charlie was going down the long slide leading to the lake. She kept getting stuck on her long journey down, but was determined to join her family already swimming in the cool lake. Comparing Charlie to the "Little Engine that Could" she tried and tried to inch down the slide, but could not. One more push and Charlie slid quickly down and landed in the lake with a huge splash.

Leila always thinks about Charlotte's perseverance. Throughout Leila's life, Charlotte inspired her and others. She passed on a sense of humor and determination. The moral of this story is: Like the Little Engine that Could said, "I think I can, I think I can" we always say "We know we can, We know we can!" We persevere through any obstacles, even when we get stuck. We push through, "We can and we will! Charlotte instilled a strong work ethic in her daughter and granddaughter. Leila wished that after forty-five years of married bliss and mother-in-law influence, this work ethic would rub off on her husband, Sheldon. Here's to hoping! Well, maybe someday it will happen.

Looking forward, we look for platforms to establish recognition and visibility. We use in-store Events, YouTube Videos, Online Sites, Amazon, and National Magazines to stay in front of our audience. We are keeping our end game in the forefront. Leila and Erika want to be visible in front of a nationwide audience. We envision our own cooking show or a talk show to highlight our mother-daughter relationship and our passions for what we do. What's the use of dreaming if you cannot reach the sky? What's that old cliché that says, "The sky's the limit"? We say don't place any limitations on what you could do— dream big. Our dream is for world domination, one scone at a time. We wish for Leila's cookbook to be in everyone's kitchen, an Erika's Tea Room scone to be on everyone's table, and a Erika's tea set and scone bundle at every celebration. As we said . . . World Domination!

ALL IN THE FAMILY (WELCOME TO THE FAMILY)

We have met many wonderful people coming through the tea room doors, online, and on the phone. While every guest is special, there are some who go beyond friendship and who we consider family. Some come into the tea room every week, and others are seasonal, but the commonality is that we see and speak to these wonderful friends often.

The word "family" means something different to different people. Family could be the people you grew up with; your immediate family. But for us, family is the people who have entered our tea room doors, and continue to be a part of our world, and have taken a place in our hearts. Our Erika's Tea Room family are people we care for and those who care for us. We are so grateful for these family members that we spend most of our time with them.

When we first opened the tea room, we invited people from the local community to taste test our recipes and do a trial run. These guinea pigs loved everything and offered very little help in deciding between one thing or the other. Most of these first visitors are still coming through the tea room doors today. Erika has reached out to more and more peeps around our vast country and Canada, honing her social media skills. Leila is ecstatic to now have these family members who have tried our scones alone and in scone bundles and keep coming back for more.

We had a local customer order scones for her son stationed in Alaska. She called us a week later and told us how her son had fallen in love with our scones. He had one each day for breakfast. The only bad thing was that our scones arrived frozen! The good news was that we included instructions of reheating our scones, even if you choose to freeze them. Our customer thought it was hysterical that the scones were frozen in her son's mailbox. Luckily our scones are prepared for every eventuality!

Now we want to tell you how we met our family and what memories we share with them. We met Fran and Jack close to nine years ago. They came to the tea room almost every Sunday after Church for an afternoon tea luncheon. Fran loved coconut, so Leila made her coconut macaroons, coconut scones, and coconut cupcakes, or even bread pudding, whenever she could. Jack loved Leila's soups and anything fish. Fran was anti-fish. Leila made tuna or shrimp sandwiches to satisfy Jack's tastes, while Fran chose from other sandwich choices. Jack and Fran also attended most of the themed events that the tea room put on. Jack and Fran became so close to the family. We shared family secrets and were great sounding boards for each other.

Jack and Fran also attended some personal dinners held in the tea room. They sat through one of our Passover dinners. They tried the Manischewitz grape wine that Jack tells us he still buys today. We read from a Haggadah and explained the ritual. Jack and Fran graciously tried the homemade chopped liver, gefilte fish, and brisket. They even ate the Matzo. Matzo is a flat unleavened bread that has very little taste. This season they introduced gluten-free matzo. Erika predicts that next season they will include plant-based matzo. (Erika is confident that this idea will make millions one day.)

Jack has been a male model for us in two of our fashion shows. He proudly struts his stuff in one of the Hawaiian shirts we were selling. Jack makes it evident that he loves the shirts, since he probably has one of each of the styles. He plays it up to the all-female audience while Fran sits there shaking her head. Jack is the best male model we ever had, especially because he was our only male model!

Jack and Fran recently moved far away from us. We might not see them as often as we would like, but they will always hold a special place in our hearts. We asked Fran and Jack to share some of their thoughts on our tea room.

By chance we were shopping in downtown Clermont and decided to stop in and enjoy a nice lunch and tea. Erika had a friendly greeting and introduced her mother, Leila, to us. We chatted with them, and we are now friends as well as regular customers. Our favorite memories include sing-along evening events. Leila makes me the best homemade soup. Another favorite is meeting Shelly, Leila's husband. We enjoy visiting with the Shanoff family.

We believe that Erika's Tea Room makes the absolute best scones. We order them to be delivered to us by mail when we are not in the area. In one word we would describe them as "Delicious". We love Erika and Leila's friendly banter and their caring for their customers. We are the living proof that they truly 'Make a memory in every cup' and that is what makes Erika's Tea Room unique. Jack and Frances

Elaine from Maine, also Florida, is one of our snowbirds. This means that she spends the winter months in Florida and the summers in Maine. Elaine is a lovely retired nurse that has become a wonderful friend. She worries about us and checks in on us from wherever she is. Elaine loves our gourmet events. This is a special event we hold by partnering with gourmet sellers that prepare bread mixes, dip mixes, biscuit mixes, honeys, apple butters, jams, pizza dough mixes, and others. Leila takes these mixes and prepares them by adding her special flare and then the attendees do the tasting. They also get additional recipes to take home and enjoy. All of the mixes are available to purchase. Elaine usually gets a lot of the mixes for holiday and birthday gifting ideas. When he is here in Florida, Elaine's husband also attends these gourmet events.

Elaine has the most laid-back personality of anyone we know. She always blames Erika for helping her spend so much money, but she keeps coming back for more. Erika always responds fondly, "I only help with healthy addictions." We all laugh as Elaine continues looking at all the new additions in the gift shop. We asked Elaine to share some of her thoughts.

Dear Erika and Leila,

Here are my contributions for your book. So hard to be brief as I love you guys so much. See you in October. Miss you. Hope all is going well. I admire you both and a big hug to your dad, Erika. He is so special and always gives me the sweetest smiles whatever he is doing. Let me start by saying that just after they opened, I walked by Erika's Tea Room and their colorful and fun storefront immediately caught my eye. I walked into a warm and welcoming environment. Being alone, they made me feel like family and I stayed for tea. The tea, the homemade scones, tea sandwiches, soups, quiches, and desserts were delicious. I ended up buying a beautiful tea set and lots of teas. Their selections are amazing. I have been returning ever since.

I have so many wonderful memories, it is impossible to pick just one. Erika's Tea Room has so many varieties of tea available, it is hard to choose. Erika and Leila are wonderful in helping you make the perfect decision every time. I love their personalized attention and care. I keep going back for their delicious shrimp, chicken, and egg salad tea sandwiches. There are many other choices, but these are my favorites. All Leila's soups are exquisite. Their staff are always so caring and helpful and remember your special requests.

Erika's Tea Room's food demo and taste classes are the best entertainment in town. And such fun! Leila teaches you about new foods and fun tasty combinations. I have learned so many cooking tricks and tips. And Leila and Erika are always so entertaining in their deliveries at these classes. My husband enjoys it as much as I do.

Erika's Tea Room's Shop is also the perfect place to purchase unique and special gifts for family and friends. They will also gift wrap, ship, and enclose scones of your choice with any gift. Makes it so easy! I would describe their scones as love in a box. Leila and Erika always make you feel like family.

Love always, Elaine

Our friend Thometra from Indiana is a special lady who we met just three years before writing this book, but she has already become part of our family. She and her husband, Pastor James, pray with us and for us and we are very grateful to have them in our lives. It was evident at the beginning that Thometra was extremely interested in learning more about tea and the tea business. Erika loves to talk about teas and is always interested in sharing her knowledge. We can say that our love for tea has brought our world and Thometra's world together. Thometra's interest in tea has led her to her new tea business. She supplies us with her personal labels and we custom blend teas for her to sell.

At the present time we are trying to make her a sweet potato tea. We can make a perfect pumpkin spice, but sweet potato is more challenging. Leila makes a mean sweet potato scone though. She just purchased sweet potato powder. This along with a good black tea foundation and spices should work. Leila and Erika will experiment with quantities to see what happens. We talk to Thometra often, sharing ideas and how things are going. It is quite wonderful to have Thometra in our lives and we appreciate having our own special tea sister in Indiana. We asked Thometra to share some of her thoughts.

I was reading my Tea Magazine. There was an advertisement from Erika's Tea Room about a Zoom tea event, so I signed up and called my tea sister/friend and she signed up too. This virtual event would be a time of fellowship for all. I was excited about the listed activities including an arts and craft project that we could do together over Zoom. We also received a featured scone and hot tea sample that complimented the scone. It was a weekly event for about six weeks. I met women from around the country. Erika and Leila also had a few 'Cooking with Tea' demonstrations. I enjoyed this special time of tea with Erika, Leila, and new friends.

My brother-in-law planned a trip to Daytona Beach, Florida, for his wife's birthday and retirement in September. My husband knew we had to go because Daytona Beach, FL, was not far from Erika's Tea Room in Clermont, FL. I was looking forward to meeting Erika and Leila in person and shopping in their Tea Room. The four of us went and had afternoon tea, which was delicious, and then we shopped in their gorgeous Tea Room store. I was so happy to finally meet them in person, along with Mr. Shanoff.

I would describe Leila's scones as Scone-licious!! Erika and Leila are both so warm and friendly. They make you feel like family. It's like you have known them all your life. They are professional, their standards are high, and they have a wealth of knowledge on this drink called TEA! Thometra

CeCe started in the tea room as our tea hostess supreme. She is so even-keeled and is not thrown by any of our tea room guests. All tea room customers love CeCe. She stays on top of their needs and is Johnny-on-the Spot in making their tea room experience special. CeCe makes a mean pot of tea. Since CeCe started making the tea, there has not been a complaint. We had previous tea hostesses that did not fare as well. Leila loves CeCe's interest in cooking and baking and asks for CeCe's assistance when trying new recipes. Leila also utilizes CeCe's great palette to be taste tester and is never disappointed with her attention to detail.

Erika appreciates CeCe's help with shipping our scones and scone bundles. CeCe maintains the labeling of the scone and tea packaging. She also helps with boxing and is a great right hand. CeCe does not mind helping any way she can and fits like a glove in our tea room. We could not pick a more wonderful addition to our family. Many people ask Erika if CeCe is her sister and Erika replies, "She is my sister from another mister." Others ask Leila if CeCe is Erika or her daughter and Leila replies, "CeCe is like another daughter to me!" We asked CeCe to share some of her thoughts.

I met Erika and Leila about three years ago when I started working for the family as a tea hostess in the tea room. My favorite memories with Erika and Leila are all the teachable moments we have shared in the kitchen with Leila and in the tea room with Erika. Those moments I will cherish for the rest of my life. I get to try all the scones and usually get all the scone runts. Leila's scones, in just one word, would be 'Perfection'. Leila and Erika put their heart and soul into everything they do.

Our friend Margaret from The Villages in Florida lives about an hour from the tea room. The first time Margaret came to the tea room, she was accompanied by a group of her neighborhood friends. Margaret is one of the most kind-hearted, considerate women that we have ever met. She always has a kind word for everyone and has a wonderful group of friends. After the first time coming to our tea room, we became immediate close friends and our tea room became a regular meeting place for Margaret's group. We have created special events, such as fashion show luncheons, for them to attend.

Erika loves to help Margaret shop. Margaret calls Erika her friendly little meatball. Erika assures her that she only helps her with healthy addictions like shopping for scones and tea pots. The two of them laugh constantly as Erika shows Margaret all the new things that just arrived. It is such a pleasure to find such a kindred spirit in Margaret and we think of her as a great addition to the family. We asked Margaret to share some of her thoughts.

Our ladies group went to Erika's Tea Room as an outing. We fell in love with the tea room. Erika, her mom Leila, and the staff were just so warm and friendly that they made us feel right at home. All my memories about the tea room are wonderful, it would be hard to pick out one specific time that was better than the next. If there was one word to describe Leila's scones, I guess it would be AWESOME!

Erika's Tea Room is just a wonderful place; from the old-fashioned China, to the table settings, to the food that is absolutely delicious. The scones are to die for. Each flavor that Leila makes, you can taste all the ingredients, they melt in your mouth. The soups, the quiches, sandwiches and then the grand finale…. the desserts. I just love being there. Erika and Leila treat you like family. It's like coming home!

Leslie came into our life three years before writing this book and immediately became a member of our family. She attends all of our events and comes several days during the week. Anytime we have boxes to open and tea pots to look at, or gift bundles to pack up, Leslie volunteers to help. Leslie makes our single guests feel welcome and often sits with them, explaining the lay of the land. Erika calls her Auntie Leslie and feels very close to her. Both Leila and Erika look at Leslie as a confidant, sharing many secrets between them. We asked Leslie to share some of her thoughts:

The first time I came to the tea room, I brought my sister with me. We thoroughly enjoyed our time at the tea room and noticed a tasting event flier on the door. I signed up that very day. Since that time, I have been coming back to all of the themed events that the tea room has to offer. I come a couple days a week to spend time with Erika and Leila, many times sharing lunch. I love these events, especially the "Mother and Daughter Act!"

The tea room has become my home away from home. It is the place for me to create new friendships. Their scones are "Scrumdiliumcious!" Mostly, I love the comradery, friendliness, and laughter we always share.

We bake and ship our scone and
gift bundles nationwide!

"Fran's Favorite" Coconut Macaroon Recipe

INGREDIENTS

1 14-ounce bag coconut flakes

1 14-ounce can sweetened condensed milk

1 teaspoon vanilla extract

½ teaspoon almond extract

2/3 cup all-purpose flour

DIRECTIONS

1. Preheat the oven to 350 degrees F.

2. Line a baking sheet with parchment paper.

3. In a large bowl with a large spoon, mix the coconut, extracts, and milk.

4. Add the flour until fully blended.

5. Using a 1-inch cookie scoop, drop the dough onto a baking sheet.

6. Bake for 12 to 15 minutes or until lightly browned.

Leila's Tasteful Tips

- You can add ¼ cup of your favorite flavor of chocolate chips.
- You can add ¼ cup of slivered almonds or another choice of nuts.

"Elaine's Favorite" Tropical Shrimp Salad Recipe

INGREDIENTS

1 24-ounce bag of frozen salad shrimp

2 Tablespoons of regular mayonnaise

2 Tablespoons of toasted coconut

1 8-ounce can of mandarin oranges (drained)

1 teaspoon of ground black pepper

1 teaspoon of garlic powder

1 teaspoon of onion powder

1 10-ounce container of fresh baby spinach (prewashed)

DIRECTIONS

1. Thaw the frozen shrimp. Place the shrimp in a colander and run cold water over them until softened.

2. Grind the shrimp in a food processor.

3. Drain the oranges and pull the segments apart with your hands.

4. In a large bowl mix the shrimp, mayonnaise, coconut, oranges, and spices.

5. Put a bed of spinach on the plate. Place a scoop of shrimp salad on the spinach and then serve.

Leila's Tasteful Tips

- Shrimp salad is wonderful on a croissant or any of your favorite breads.
- To make a classic shrimp salad, omit the oranges and coconut and add 2 stalks of chopped celery and 1 Tablespoon of chives.

"Thometra's Favorite" Sweet Potato Green Tea Recipe

INGREDIENTS

1-ounce of green tea from Japan

2 Tablespoons of dried sweet potato buds

1 teaspoon of ground cinnamon

1 teaspoon of ground nutmeg

DIRECTIONS

1. Mix the sweet potato buds and spices into the green tea.

2. Steep a heaping teaspoon of tea in 8-ounces of boiling water.

3. Steep for three to five minutes and then enjoy your cup of tea.

"Margaret's Favorite" Baked Potato Soup Recipe

INGREDIENTS

2 32-ounce containers of chicken stock

1 28-ounce bag of frozen tater tots

1 12-ounce bag of frozen diced onions

1 12-ounce bag of frozen carrots

1 cup of heavy cream

2 teaspoons of each – ground black pepper, onion powder, and garlic powder

DIRECTIONS

1. In a 5-quart stew pot put the chicken stock, the onions, the carrots and the spices. Stir to mix all the ingredients.

2. Bring the soup to a boil and then turn the temperature down to low.

3. Add tater tots and heavy cream.

4. Continue stirring until the tater tots are infused into the soup.

5. Taste to see if the soup has enough spices. Add a little more spice if needed.

6. Then the soup is ready to serve.

Leila's Tasteful Tips

- You can top the soup with shredded cheddar cheese.
- You can also top with bacon bits.

"Leslie's Favorite" Broccoli Potato Quiche Recipe

INGREDIENTS

1 12-ounce bag of frozen steamable broccoli

1 15-ounce can of diced potatoes

2 Tablespoons of canola oil

2 teaspoons of each – ground black pepper, garlic powder, and onion powder

2 teaspoons of paprika

1 8-ounce bag of shredded triple cheddar cheese

1 frozen 9-inch deep dish pie shell (do not defrost)

6 large eggs

1 pint of half and half or heavy cream

DIRECTIONS

1. Preheat the oven to 375 degrees F.

2. In a colander drain the diced potatoes and rinse.

3. Coat the potatoes with the oil and 1 teaspoon of each of the spices. Add paprika.

4. Place the potatoes in a baking dish and bake for 15 minutes. Allow to cool.

5. Steam the frozen broccoli for 6 minutes.

6. Open onto a paper towel. When cool, cut into small pieces. Set aside.

7. In a large bowl whisk the eggs with the half and half (or heavy cream)

8. Whisk in 1 teaspoon of the three spices.

9. Mix the cooled potatoes, the broccoli, and the shredded cheese.

10. Spread evenly in the frozen pie shell.

11. Pour the egg mixture over the top of the potatoes, broccoli, and cheese. Keeping ¼ cup to cover edges.

12. Bake for 20 to 30 minutes or until browned.

13. Makes 6 to 8 slices.

Leila's Tasteful Tips

- You can use any other frozen steamable vegetable of your choice.

- You can use any other shredded cheese of your choice.

- Instead of diced potatoes in a can, you can use shredded hash brown potatoes.

- You can sprinkle grated parmesan cheese over the individual slices for an elevated taste.

- Cover the pie shell rim with the egg mixture to prevent it from cracking when you are making slices. The egg mixture thickens the pie crust, so when you slice it, you do not lose any of the crust's yummy goodness!

"CeCe's Favorite" Baked Tomato Pie Recipe

INGREDIENTS

1 large beefsteak tomato

1 8-ounce fresh mozzarella cheese ball (pre-sliced)

2 Tablespoons extra virgin olive oil

1 Tablespoon balsamic vinegar

1 teaspoon garlic powder

1 teaspoon onion powder

1 teaspoon ground black pepper

1 teaspoon oregano

1 whole Italian bread

Baking spray

DIRECTIONS

1. Preheat the oven to 375 degrees F.

2. Wash and dry the tomato and cut out the center stem.

3. Cut the tomato into thin slices.

4. Cut the bread into ½ inch thick slices.

5. Whisk the olive oil, balsamic vinegar, and spices.

6. Using a pastry brush, brush each tomato and each bread slice with the oil mixture.

7. Spray a baking pan with baking spray.

8. Place the bread on the bottom of the baking pan, filling in all the spaces.

9. Place the basted tomato slices on top of the bread.

10. Bake for 15 to 20 minutes or until tomatoes are softened.

11. Add the fresh mozzarella cheese on the top and return to the oven for an additional 10 minutes or until the cheese is melted.

12. Make slices and serve.

SCONE PROVERBS AND JOKES TO LIVE BY

Leila and Erika might actually be idiot savants. We are on our own level. In fact, no one else would want to be on our level! We are so passionate and involved in what we do that it encompasses everything in our lives. We laugh constantly, making the most out of life and our love for what we do.

Since scones are so much a part of our daily business, we would like to share some wandering thoughts. . .

- What happened when the scone crossed the road? It got creamed. . .
- Where is my cream and jam? Don't worry, it's only a scone's throw away!
- I like big scones, and I just can't lie!
- A scone a day keeps the doctor away! Have you had a scone today?
- Knock, knock. Who's there? Devon Cream! Knock, knock. Who's there? Jelly. Knock, knock. Who's there? Scone. Scone who? How can you have a scone without cream and jelly!
- Friends are like scones, you can never have too many!
- All roads lead to scones!
- Stop and smell the scones!
- Scones - it's what's for dinner!
- Move over cookies. . . Eat scones! What goes better with milk?
- Life's short, eat your scones first!

- Plan your daily menu sconefully! Breakfast – scone. Lunch- scone. Dinner- scone. Got it!

- There's a new movie coming out this fall. It's called "Romancing the Scone". It's rated PD – positively delicious!

- The old lady's two nasty parrots died after she gave them a bit of her scone. When asked what happened she replied, "I killed two birds with one scone!"

- Erika was in the kitchen making scones. She was covered with flour, egg, cream, and butter. Leila asked Erika what had happened. Erika replied, "Hell hath no fury like a woman sconed!"

See, Leila told you there is a method to her madness. Stop sconing around and tell a good scone joke!

LIVE FROM ERIKA'S TEA ROOM

Both Leila and Erika grew up watching theatrics both in the theater and on TV. We love to entertain the people entering our doors. It is so evident that our mother-daughter interactions are very funny. Erika makes fun of Leila's New York accent. Leila asks, "I dunno what she means! What's wrong with the word Octoba?" The dynamic duo poke fun at each other, keep each other on our toes, and keep customers laughing. We play off each other. Leila makes a statement such as, "I can picture Erika in the kitchen baking scones. I see flour everywhere, scones nowhere!" Erika comes back with, "I can do anything my mother can do. I just choose not to!"

In the tea room we love to say, "We laugh-ed, we joke-ed, we ran amuck, amuck, amuck, amuck!" There are two ways to work: with or without fun and laughter. No matter what we do, we want to share some laughter with everyone we meet. Erika calls Leila the one-take wonder. It's just like Leila's sister's violin recitals: she played the wrong notes and kept right on going. We might make mistakes, but we keep on going. Most of the time we make fun of each other, but always in a playful way.

When Erika wants to feature a new bundle, a new item to be purchased, or one that just arrived, or even a new flavor of scone, she calls upon Leila's talents. Leila literally takes down her hair, puts on some lipstick, and poses for the camera – or should we say Erika's iPhone. Leila tells Erika to only shoot her good side; Erika is still looking for it.

When we decided to do live videos, it was just an extension of our daily routine. There was no rehearsal or notes written; we love spontaneity. We would love to be on a reality cooking and baking show where we interact with the audience. In our videos, as usual, we are bonding on the air; playing off each other's sentences and thoughts. We never know who will come up with a unique thought, and then the other will run with that thought and take it in an unexpected direction!

Our videos started with snip-its from our themed events, adding videos from the kitchen creating recipes for the themed events, and also reboots of menu items from visiting other tearooms. Leila especially loves live videos where she can interact with viewers, answering questions, and sharing Leila's Tasty Tips. Erika posts to many social media channels to show off our talents. There is the good, the bad, and mostly the ugly. We are not sure which category or categories we fall into. But as they say, you cannot keep a good man down, or instead, a good woman down, and we will continue making our humorous videos for all to enjoy!

OUR FUTURE, WHAT TO EXPECT IN THE NEXT CHAPTER

The ending or the beginning . . . This is where the optimist in Leila meets the pessimist in Erika head on. No one can predict what will happen in the future. There are things we definitely know and then there's the unexpected. What we do know is that our story is not over yet and we cannot wait to see what the next chapter holds. You might ask where do you want to be when you grow up? Leila would say, anywhere that Erika is. In all modesty, we are looking for world domination and, of course, world peace. But in all sincerity, we will settle for every person on earth sitting down to a wonderful cuppa tea with one of our varieties of scones.

Our story is not going to end here. We have more scones to bake, more teapots to sell, more recipes to create, and more memories to share. We wish all of you good scones, good tea, and good friends. All of which you can find at Erika's Tea Room. See you soon!

www.ingramcontent.com/pod-product-compliance
Lightning Source LLC
Chambersburg PA
CBHW040246100426
42811CB00011B/1175